365 Days of Pause & Abundance

Practical Daily Tips & Wisdom

By

KIM GROSHEK

An imprint of Creatively Canny Publishing

Printed in the U.S.A.
ISBN- 978-1-942604-67-9

My Lovely Daughter

I would never wish for my daughter to be anything other than exactly who she is. She is bright, kind, sensitive, and deeply caring—a genuinely conscientious and good person. She has a heart full of empathy and a mind rich with creativity, making her a gifted writer and communicator. Her words have the power to move, inspire, and connect, and that is a gift beyond measure. What more could a parent ask for in their child? I have been truly blessed. While every parent sees their child as unique, I know deep in my heart that Staci possesses a light that shines uniquely and beautifully. She is thoughtful, intuitive, and filled with a quiet strength that makes the world a better place just by being in it. My only wish for my daughter is that she continues to experience a life full of love, happiness, joy, and fulfillment—both creatively and personally. May she always embrace the brilliance within her, follow her dreams with passion, and never doubt how deeply she is loved.

You are a gift. Keep shining. 💖

Foreword

Interacting with Kim is a breath of fresh air. After decades of training and experience as a Personal Transformation facilitator and course creator, I have reached the pinnacle of my field, so people often don't challenge my ideas or intentions, allowing me to move through life with a sense of certainty that can sometimes border on complacency. But Kim has a rare gift—she can nudge me out of the fixed ideas I've held onto, many of which I've grown accustomed to over the years, even though they are no longer relevant in the rapidly evolving market I now find myself in.

She effortlessly disrupts my thinking and reminds me that growth comes not from holding tightly to what's comfortable but from embracing new ways of thinking and being.

In every interaction, Kim gets my creative juices flowing in ways I never expected. Her brilliance lies in her ability to illuminate the blind spots we often overlook, whether we are consciously aware of them or not. She challenges me to see things differently, breaking down barriers that prevent me from seeing the broader, in-depth planetary picture. Through her guidance, I've been able to reimagine my approach, recalibrate my intentions, and ultimately create more impactful transformations in the work I do.

If you are a teacher, a trainer, a leader, or an agent of transformation, you may resonate with the feeling that people often agree with you rather than challenge your perspectives. It's easy to feel secure in your expertise and forget that even the most seasoned professionals can become limited by their assumptions. Kim Groshek possesses an extraordinary ability to perceive and confront the limiting beliefs that may be holding you back, pushing you to explore your blind spots and plunge into the discomfort of growth.

Kim's work goes beyond conventional boundaries. She asks tough questions, presents unsettling truths, and invites readers to explore the hidden forces and systems that influence our daily lives in ways we rarely consider. 365 Days of Pause & Abundance is a powerful testament to her passion for awakening individuals. This book is not just a reflection of Kim's profound insights into the world today; it's an invitation to reclaim our power and challenge the structures that have conditioned us to believe in systems that serve only the few rather than the many.

Kim's unique perspective and vision will undoubtedly leave you questioning long-held assumptions, rethinking your place in a world of manipulation, and empowering you to create change in your life and beyond.

As you dive into this book, be prepared to see the world through a different lens. The insights to practice within these pages are not just thought-provoking—they are transformative. They will stir your emotions and inspire you to take action to reclaim your autonomy, purpose, and power.

Marianne Torrence, Personal Transformation Facilitator & Course Creator

Preface

In a world that glorifies hustle and constant movement, we often forget that true abundance comes not from doing more but from pausing with intention. **365 Days of Pause & Abundance** is an invitation to step back, reflect, and reconnect with what truly matters—your purpose, your vision, and the limitless potential within you.

As an entrepreneur, leader, or creative thinker, you are constantly making decisions, innovating, and striving for success. But what if the key to achieving more wasn't pushing harder but pausing smarter? This book is designed to help you cultivate **intentional pauses**—moments of stillness that spark clarity, resilience, and inspired action.

Each day, you'll find **practical tips, mindset shifts, and entrepreneurial wisdom** that empower you to:

- Reignite your creativity and focus
- Align your daily actions with your long-term vision
- Strengthen your mindset for sustainable success
- Build habits that foster both wealth and well-being
- Find joy in the journey, not just the destination.

With just **15 minutes a day**, you can shift from feeling overwhelmed to operating from a place of **purpose, balance, and abundance**. Whether you're starting your morning with intention, resetting midday, or winding down in reflection, these daily practices will support you in creating a life and business that thrives—without burnout. Your success is not just about **what you do** but also about **how you**

pause. So take a breath, embrace the wisdom within these pages, and let's embark on a year of transformation—one intentional pause at a time.

With gratitude and abundance, Kim Groshek

Introduction

It's easy to feel like success comes from constantly moving, doing, and achieving. But what if the real key to success is not in the rush—but in the pause? Science, psychology, and the wisdom of top entrepreneurs reveal that taking intentional moments to pause leads to greater clarity, creativity, and impact.

Why Pausing Matters: The Science Behind Mindfulness and Success

Pausing isn't just about relaxation—it's a **performance strategy** backed by neuroscience. Research shows that brief moments of mindfulness improve focus, enhance decision-making, and reduce stress. The brain needs space to process information, and when we intentionally step back, we allow insights to emerge.

From a physiological standpoint, pausing activates the **parasympathetic nervous system**, which helps regulate stress and improve overall well-being. This is why **leaders, athletes, and high achievers** incorporate mindful reflection into their routines. Pausing creates **mental resilience, emotional intelligence, and strategic thinking**, all essential for long-term success.

How to Use This Guide: Morning, Noon, Evening Pauses + Classroom Practices

This guide is designed to **help you integrate daily pauses**—in just a few minutes each morning, noon, and evening. Each pause serves a distinct purpose:

- **Morning Pause** – Start your day with intention,

clarity, and gratitude.

- **Noon Pause** – Reset and refocus, ensuring your energy remains aligned with your goals.
- **Evening Pause** – Reflect, release stress, and prepare your mind for restful sleep.

For students in the classroom, these pauses are structured to **enhance learning, creativity, and leadership**. Designed for **young adults**, the exercises foster self-awareness, discipline, and an abundance mindset—key qualities for future success. By incorporating these pauses, students not only improve academic performance but also develop **mental clarity, resilience, and emotional intelligence**.

Developing an Abundance Mindset: The Role of Pausing in Business, Leadership, and Life

An **abundance mindset** is a belief that **opportunities, creativity, and success are limitless**. It's the opposite of scarcity thinking, where fear and competition dominate. Entrepreneurs and business leaders who cultivate an abundance mindset make **better decisions, collaborate more effectively, and recognize opportunities others miss**.

Pausing plays a critical role in shifting from **scarcity to abundance**. Instead of reacting out of fear, pausing allows time to **reset perspectives, reframe challenges, and generate creative solutions**. This is how **visionaries build lasting success**—not through frantic action but through strategic reflection.

The Connection Between Pausing & Success: How Top Entrepreneurs Use Reflection to Create Impact

The world's most successful individuals—**Oprah Winfrey, Warren Buffett, Bill Gates, and Arianna Huffington**—all incorporate **deliberate pauses** into their lives—
Oprah journals daily, using reflection to maintain clarity and purpose. **Warren Buffett** spends 80% of his time thinking rather than constantly making decisions. **Bill Gates** takes "Think Weeks" to pause and generate innovative ideas. **Arianna Huffington** advocates for rest and reflection as essential to peak performance.

This guide is your **blueprint for integrating mindful pauses into your life and work**. By following these simple daily practices, you will develop greater clarity, creativity, resilience, and a deep sense of abundance.

It's time to stop rushing and start pausing—because **the most successful people don't just work harder; they think smarter.**

Are you ready to transform your life through the power of pause? Let's begin.

Daily Structure

Consistently pausing throughout the day helps you maintain a clear, focused mind and fosters a sense of peace and productivity. These daily practices help you stay aligned with your intentions and grow personally and professionally.

Each day includes:

- ✓ **Morning Pause (5 min):** Centering and setting intentions. Start the day grounded and focused on your purpose and goals.
- ✓ **Noon Pause (5-10 min):** Reset and refocus for clarity. Take a break to clear your mind, refresh your energy, and regain focus.
- ✓ **Evening Pause (3-5 min):** Reflection and gratitude practice. Wind down by reflecting on the day's highlights and expressing gratitude.
- ✓ **Classroom Practice (for students 15-18):** A structured daily or weekly exercise – Engage in focused exercises to build mindfulness and deepen understanding of each day's lessons.
- ✓ **Daily Abundance Quote:** Wisdom from entrepreneurs, business owners, and influencers – Gain insight and inspiration from the words of leaders who embody the abundance mindset.

Monthly Themes & Weekly Classroom Structure

We will explore a central theme each month, and each week will feature specific activities designed to deepen classroom practice. These themes and exercises will help students cultivate resilience, sharpen focus, and develop an abundance mindset to guide their academic and personal success.

The Power of Pause & Intention

The **Power of Pause & Intention** is the foundation for creating a life of mindfulness, focus, and success. By incorporating small yet intentional pauses throughout the day, you cultivate clarity, reduce stress, and enhance decision-making.

- ✓ **Week 1:** Introduction to the Pause Habit (morning/noon/night) – Establish the practice of pausing and setting mindful intentions throughout the day.
- ✓ **Week 2:** Breathing techniques to center yourself – Learn simple yet powerful breathwork exercises to stay calm, focused, and present.
- ✓ **Week 3:** Visualizing your best day ahead – Use visualization techniques to prepare for a productive and fulfilling day mentally.
- ✓ **Week 4:** The role of clarity in success – Explore how pausing for clarity leads to better choices, more decisive leadership, and greater fulfillment.

By the end of this month, you will have built a **solid foundation of mindful pausing**, which will help you approach each day with greater purpose and presence.

Introduction to the Pause Habit

Incorporating small, mindful pauses throughout the day helps create a sense of balance, presence, and mental clarity.

These simple yet effective practices allow you to reset, refocus, and build a habit of mindfulness.

- ✓ **Morning:** Simple breathing exercises to start the day. Deep breathing awakens the mind and sets a calm, intentional tone.
- ✓ **Noon:** Do a quick body scan to notice the tension—check-in with your body to release any built-up stress and restore focus.
- ✓ **Evening:** Reflect on a moment of pause. Take time to acknowledge moments of stillness and how they impacted your day.
- ✓ **Classroom Activity: Silent Start Challenge**—Begin class with 2 minutes of stillness, and discuss how this impacts focus and learning.

By practicing these small pauses, you'll develop greater self-awareness, resilience, and the ability to navigate each day with more ease and intention.

Part One

Day 1

The Power of Stillness – Recharging Through Pause

Morning: Set intentions with deep breathing (inhale for 4, hold for 4, exhale for 4).

Afternoon: Notice new opportunities with a head-to-toe body scan, releasing tension.

Evening: Reflect on a moment when you intentionally paused today.

Classroom Activity: *Silent Start Challenge* – Begin class with 2 minutes of stillness, then discuss its impact on focus and awareness.

Almost everything will work again if you unplug it for a few minutes, including you. – Anne Lamott

Day 2

Embracing Change Through Mindful Pauses

Morning: Set an intention with the affirmation: *"I move through today with ease and clarity."*

Afternoon: Stretch and take three deep breaths before continuing work.

Evening: Write down one lesson learned from the day.

Classroom Activity: *Mindful Observation* – Spend 5 minutes noticing details in the classroom and sharing insights.

"Pause. Breathe. Repair your universe, then proceed." – Kim Groshek.

Day 3

Cultivating Calm Through Mindful Awareness

Morning: Visualize a peaceful moment from your past to cultivate calm.

Noon: Take a mindful walk, noticing sights, sounds, and sensations.

Evening: List three small wins from today.

Classroom Activity: Guided Visualization – Students close their eyes and imagine a stress-free scenario.

"Sometimes the most productive thing you can do is relax." – Mark Black

Day 4

The Power of Gratitude and Reflection

Morning: Light a candle or focus on a calming object for 2 minutes.

Noon: Take a one-minute gratitude break, thinking of things you appreciate.

Evening: Reflect on something positive that happened today.

Classroom Activity: Gratitude Circle – Each student shares one thing they're grateful for.

"A pause gives you the opportunity to reset, reflect, and reimagine your path forward" – Kim Groshek.

Day 5

Embracing Excitement and Kindness Through Pauses

Morning: Write one thing you're excited about today.

Afternoon: Listen to calming music for 5 minutes.

Evening: Journal one way you showed kindness today.

Classroom Activity: *Kindness Reflection* – Write about how pausing has impacted your week.

"Pause. Breathe. Shine." – Kim Groshek

Day 6

Reset – Reflect and Recharge

Morning: Reflect on the week so far and set an intention for the days ahead.

Noon: Engage in a mindful activity (walking, coloring, or meditating).

Evening: Share a moment of gratitude with a loved one.

Classroom Activity:

Each day is a chance to reset, reflect, and recharge. Embrace the pause, and let it guide you toward clarity and renewal." – Kim Groshek.

Day 7

Digital Detox – The Gift of Presence

Morning: *Begin the day without screens*—enjoy a quiet moment, stretch, or journal.

Afternoon: Take a mindful break by stepping outside or engaging in a hands-on activity without digital distractions.

Evening: Disconnect from devices an hour before bed and reflect on how being present enriched your day.

Classroom Activity & Today: Take a digital detox for an hour and notice how you feel.

"Pause to be." – Kim Groshek.

Day 8

Awakening Awareness Through Breath and Senses

Morning: Practice box breathing (inhale for 4 sec, hold for 4 sec, exhale for 4 sec, hold for 4 sec).

Noon: Take a 5-minute mindful break with your eyes closed, focusing on sounds around you.

Evening: Write down one moment where you felt fully present today.

Classroom Activity: Sensory Awareness – Students describe an object using all five senses.

"Pause. Breathe. Align." – *Kim Groshek*

Day 9

Focused Living – Directing Energy with Intention

Morning: Recite a positive mantra: "I am calm, centered, and focused."

Noon: Do a single-task activity with complete attention.

Evening: Reflect on something new you noticed today.

Classroom Activity: Focus Challenge – Time students for a 3-minute focus task without distractions.

Where focus goes, energy flows. – Tony Robbins

Day 10

The Art of Slowing Down – Moving with Mindfulness

Morning: Start the day with 5 slow, deep breaths before getting out of bed.

Noon: Stand up, stretch, and take 10 slow steps, noticing how each feels.

Evening: Write down one thing that brought joy today.

Classroom Activity: Walking Meditation – Students take slow, deliberate steps in silence.

When walking, walk. When eating, eat. – Zen Proverb

Day 11

Savoring the Present – Engaging the Senses

Morning: Close your eyes and focus on three sounds around you.

Noon: Take a mindful sip of tea, coffee, or water, savoring it fully.

Evening: Journal how slowing down impacted your day.

Classroom Activity: Mindful Eating – Each student takes one bite and describes the experience.

Savor the moments that are warm and special and giggly. – Sammy Davis Jr.

Day 12

Cultivating Connection Through Gratitude and Presence

Morning: Smile in the mirror and take a deep breath before starting the day.

Noon: Pause and acknowledge a co-worker or friend with full presence.

Evening: Write down three things that went well this week.

Classroom Activity: Partner Appreciation – Students express gratitude to a classmate.

Happiness is not something ready-made. It comes from your own actions. – Dalai Lama

Day 13

Weekend Reflection – Embracing Creativity and Peace

Morning: Set a weekend intention of peace and relaxation.

Noon: Do a creative activity mindfully (drawing, writing, or music).

Evening: Reflect on how pausing has changed your week.

Classroom Activity:

When you pause with intention, you create space for creativity, clarity, and peace. – Kim Groshek

Day 14

Nature's Pause – Unplug and Reconnect

Morning: Step outside and take a few deep breaths, noticing the sounds around you.

Afternoon: Take a short walk or sit quietly in nature, observing without distraction.

Evening: Reflect on how being in nature made you feel today.

Classroom Activity: *Nature's Pause Journaling* – After time outdoors, reflect on how nature's sights, sounds, and smells impacted your thoughts and feelings, fostering peace or mindfulness.

"*In the stillness of nature, we find the rhythm of our peace.*" – Kim Groshek.

Day 15

Mindful Presence – Enhancing Everyday Interactions

Morning: Start the day with mindful stretching, noticing sensations in the body.

Noon: Take a break from screens and focus on your breath for 5 minutes.

Evening: Reflect on how presence impacted your interactions today.

Classroom Activity: *Mindful Listening* – Pair up and practice active listening without interrupting.

Mindfulness isn't difficult. We need to remember to do it. – Sharon Salzberg

Day 16

Deep Appreciation – Honoring Yourself and the Moment

Morning: Write down three things you appreciate about yourself.

Noon: Eat one meal in complete silence, savoring every bite.

Evening: Journal about a time today when you felt truly present.

Classroom Activity: Silent Reflection – 3 minutes of silent journaling on a topic of choice.

Do every act of your life as though it were the last act of your life. – Marcus Aurelius

Day 17

Kindness in Action – Small Gestures, Big Impact

Morning: Begin the day with five slow, mindful breaths before speaking.

Noon: Take a mindful walk, noticing the rhythm of your steps.

Evening: Write down one moment of kindness you gave or received today.

Classroom Activity: Gratitude Notes – Write and share a short gratitude note with a classmate.

The little things? The little moments? They aren't little. – Jon Kabat-Zinn

Day 18

Emotional Awareness – Tuning Into Your Inner World

Morning: Spend 2 minutes observing your surroundings without distraction.

Noon: Pause to check in with your emotions and name what you're feeling.

Evening: Reflect on one thing you'd like to improve tomorrow.

Classroom Activity: *Emotional Check-In* – Students share how they feel using one word.

Awareness is like the sun. When it shines on things, they are transformed. – Thich Nhat Hanh

Day 19

Grounded Gratitude – Embrace the Power of Appreciation

Morning: Begin the day with a grounding exercise, feeling your feet on the floor.

Noon: Take a moment to appreciate a co-worker, classmate, or friend.

Evening: Write down three things that went well this week.

Classroom Activity: Partner Appreciation – Express gratitude to a peer.

Pause, embrace change, and step boldly into your future. – Kim Groshek

Day 20

Reflection: Embracing Presence and Joy

Morning: Practice a simple breathing meditation for 5 minutes.

Noon: Engage in a hobby with entire presence and enjoyment.

Evening: Reflect on moments of joy and laughter from the week.

Classroom Activity: *Joyful Journaling* – Have students write about a moment of pure joy or laughter this week, reflecting on how being present enhanced their happiness and connection.

Reflection enriches the soul, sparking growth through the joy of now. – Kim Groshek

Day 21

Embracing Nature's Flow

Morning: Align with nature's rhythm through a deep breath.

Afternoon: Observe the movement of wind, water, or wildlife.

Evening: Reflect on how nature's flow can inspire ease in your life.

Classroom Activity: Nature's Flow Observation – Have students observe nature's movement for 10-15 minutes and reflect on how to bring this sense of flow into their daily routines.

When we move with nature, we move with grace. – Kim Groshek.

Day 22

The Power of Intention

Morning: Set a clear intention for the day and visualize success.

Noon: Step outside for 5 minutes and observe your surroundings.

Evening: Reflect on how your intention shaped your day.

Classroom Activity: Vision Board – Create a mini vision board reflecting personal goals.

Your intention creates your reality. – Wayne Dyer

Day 23

Goal-Setting for Success

Morning: Take a moment to stretch and feel gratitude for your body.

Noon: Write down one goal and the first step to achieve it.

Evening: Journal about progress toward your goal.

Classroom Activity: Goal Setting – Students set a short-term goal and outline steps to achieve it.

A goal properly set is halfway reached. – Zig Ziglar

Day 24

Affirming Your Potential

Morning: Breathe deeply and repeat a personal affirmation.

Noon: Take a mindful break, focusing only on your breath.

Evening: Identify a moment where you acted with intention.

Classroom Activity: Positive Affirmations – Students create and share their affirmations.

We are what we repeatedly do. Excellence, then, is not an act but a habit. – Aristotle

Day 25

Mindful Responses & Gratitude

Morning: Begin with a gratitude practice, listing three things you're thankful for.

Noon: Pause before responding to a challenging situation.

Evening: Reflect on how mindfulness affected your responses today.

Classroom Activity: Mindful Decision-Making – Discuss how being intentional helps make better choices.

Live less out of habit and more out of intent. – Unknown

Day 26

The Impact of a Single Word

Morning: Set a one-word intention for the day.

Noon: Take a mindful pause before your next activity.

Evening: Reflect on how your one-word intention shaped your actions.

Classroom Activity: One-Word Challenge – Students select one word to guide their week.

Clarity comes from action, not thought. – Marie Forleo

Day 27

Aligning Intentions with Values

Morning: Spend 5 minutes meditating on your intentions.

Noon: Engage in an activity that aligns with your values.

Evening: Write a letter to your future self.

Classroom Activity: Students create a visual map linking core values to intentions, identifying aligned goals and reflecting on how they guide progress.

Let your actions mirror core intentions and values, guiding your path like an unfailing compass. – Kim Groshek

Day 28

Planning with Purpose

Morning: Set an intention for the day by identifying one purpose-driven goal.

Afternoon: Reflect on how your current actions align with your goals.

Evening: Review your day and make any necessary adjustments to stay aligned with your purpose.

Classroom Activity: Purposeful Goal Mapping – Students write a long-term goal, break it into steps, and reflect on how daily actions align with their purpose.

Your life is your message. Be intentional with it. – Mahatma Gandhi

Day 29

Cultivating Self-Compassion

Morning. Set an intention to be kind to yourself today.

Noon: Pause and place a hand on your heart, reminding yourself that you are enough.

Evening: Reflect on one moment where you showed yourself kindness.

Classroom Activity: Self-Compassion Letters – Write a letter to yourself as if you were a supportive friend.

Talk to yourself like someone you love. – Brené Brown

Day 30

Celebrating Small Wins

Morning: Take three deep breaths and smile at yourself.

Noon: Write down one small achievement from today.

Evening: Express gratitude for something you appreciate about yourself.

Classroom Activity: Celebrate Small Wins – Students list accomplishments from the past week.

Do the best you can until you know better. Then, when you know better, do better. – Maya Angelou.

Day 31

Embracing Self-Worth

Morning: Meditate on the phrase "I am worthy."

Noon: Do something enjoyable just for yourself.

Evening: Journal about what self-compassion means to you.

Classroom Activity: Self-Worth Affirmation Exercise – Students write three affirmations, repeat one daily, and reflect on its impact, followed by a discussion on how self-worth enhances confidence and overcomes challenges.

Self-worth is not defined by what you do but by who you are. Embrace your value, and the world will reflect it to you.– Kim Groshek

Day 32

Cultivating Self-Care

Morning: Set a self-care goal for the upcoming week.

Afternoon: Take a moment to check in with your energy levels and adjust accordingly.

Evening: Reflect on a tiny act of self-care you gave yourself today.

Classroom Activity: Self-Care Circle – Students share one self-care focus for the week and a new habit, then pair up to reflect on how self-care nurtures well-being and strengthens relationships.

How you love yourself is how you teach others to love you. – Rupi Kaur

Day 33

Overcoming Self-Doubt

Morning: Set a mantra: "I am capable and strong."

Noon: Recall a past challenge you overcame.

Evening: Reflect on one thing you learned today.

Classroom Activity: Confidence Collage – Create a visual board of strengths and accomplishments.

Doubt kills more dreams than failure ever will. – Suzy Kassem

Day 34

Building Confidence & Positivity

Morning: Practice power posing for 2 minutes.

Noon: Replace one negative thought with a positive affirmation.

Evening: Write down a time when you proved yourself wrong.

Classroom Activity: Positive Self-Talk – Discuss the impact of self-belief.

Believe you can, and you're halfway there. – Theodore Roosevelt

Day 35

Embracing Imperfection & Growth

Morning: Set an intention to embrace imperfections.

Noon: Take a mindful pause to acknowledge progress, not just results.

Evening: Identify a moment where you overcame a fear.

Classroom Activity: Growth Mindset Discussion – Share stories of learning from mistakes.

Perfection is the enemy of progress. – Winston Churchill

Day 36

Recognizing Your Strengths

Morning: Name three personal strengths.

Noon: Recall a compliment you received and fully accept it.

Evening: Reflect on how your strengths supported you today.

Classroom Activity: Strengths Inventory – Students identify their top three strengths.

Strength doesn't come from what you can do. It comes from overcoming things you thought you couldn't. – Rikki Rogers

Day 37

Stepping Outside Your Comfort Zone

Morning: Write down one way you will step out of your comfort zone today.

Noon: Take a short break to do something that excites you.

Evening: Celebrate the courage it took to try something new.

Classroom Activity: Comfort Zone Challenge – Encourage students to do something new and reflect on it.

Everything you've ever wanted is on the other side of fear. – George Addair

Day 38

Reflecting on Past Successes

Morning: Meditate on your past successes.

Noon: Engage in a self-care practice.

Evening: Write a letter to your future confident self.

Classroom Activity: Reflecting on Past Successes

Pause to reflect on your journey—your past successes hold the keys to your future greatness.

Day 39

Strengthening Self-Confidence

Morning: Set an intention and plan three confidence-boosting actions.

Afternoon: Step outside your comfort zone with a tiny action.

Evening: Reflect on a moment of strength and capability.

Classroom: Share confidence-building plans and uplift each other with affirmations.

"Confidence grows through intentional action." – Kim Groshek.

Day 40

Developing Resilience

Morning: Set an intention to embrace challenges with strength.

Noon: Take a deep breath and remind yourself of a past hardship you overcame.

Evening: Reflect on one lesson you learned from a demanding experience.

Classroom Activity: Students map out past challenges and how they overcame them.

Do not judge me by my success. Judge me by how many times I fell and got back up again. – Nelson Mandela

Day 41

Cultivating a Growth Mindset

Morning: Repeat a positive affirmation about learning.

Afternoon: Identify a small mistake and reframe it as a learning opportunity.

Evening: Journal one success from today, no matter how small.

Classroom Activity: Write one thing you learned today and share it with a partner.

Success is not final; failure is not fatal; it is the courage to continue that counts. – Winston Churchill

Day 42

Embracing Growth & Change

Morning: Take 5 deep breaths and set an intention for growth.

Afternoon: Try something new outside your comfort zone.

Evening: Reflect on a challenge and what it taught you.

Classroom Activity: Students discuss one time they struggled but kept going.

Challenges are what make life interesting, and overcoming them is what makes life meaningful. – Joshua J. Marine

Day 43

Embracing Growth & Change

Morning: List three qualities you admire in yourself.

Afternoon: Focus on the process of learning rather than results.

Evening: Write about how you responded to a challenge today.

Classroom Activity: Draw or write about a goal you want to achieve.

If you find a path with no obstacles, it probably doesn't lead anywhere. – Frank A. Clark

Day 44

The Power of Persistence

Morning: Visualize yourself succeeding in a personal challenge.

Afternoon: Share a piece of knowledge with a friend.

Evening: Reflect on how effort and persistence shaped your day.

Classroom Activity: Write letters to your future self about your goals.

Do not be embarrassed by your failures; learn from them and start again. – Richard Branson

Day 45

Breaking Free from Limiting Beliefs

Morning: Start the day by saying, "I am capable and resilient."

Afternoon: Identify one obstacle and brainstorm ways to overcome it.

Evening: Write about one improvement you noticed today.

Classroom Activity: Pair up and give each other one piece of positive feedback.

Believe you can and you're halfway there. - Theodore Roosevelt

Day 46

Overcoming Limiting Beliefs

Morning: Identify one limiting belief and write its opposite.

Afternoon: Think of a time you proved a doubt wrong.

Evening: Reflect on what new belief you want to adopt.

Classroom Activity: Group discussion on self-imposed limitations and how to challenge them.

Your only limit is your mind. – Kim Groshek

Day 47

Embracing Limitless Potential

Morning: Say aloud, "I am limitless and capable."

Afternoon: Try a task you've been avoiding.

Evening: List three things you did today that proved your strength.

Classroom Activity: Role-play overcoming a fear or challenge.

Whether you think you can or you think you can't—you're right. – Henry Ford

Day 48

Conquering Fear

Morning: Write down a fear and a reason why it's not true.

Afternoon: Tackle a small step toward overcoming a fear.

Evening: Journal about how it felt to push past a limiting belief.

Classroom Activity: Create a positive mantra to replace a common fear.

Doubt kills more dreams than failure ever will. – Suzy Kassem

Day 49

Turning Failures Into Lessons

Morning: Reflect on how you react to setbacks.

Afternoon: Find an opportunity in a past failure.

Evening: Write down one thing you learned today that surprised you.

Classroom Activity: Discuss a time when failure led to success.

Failure is simply the opportunity to begin again, this time more intelligently. – Henry Ford

Day 50

The Power of an Open Mind

Morning: Set an intention to stay open-minded today.

Afternoon: Seek advice from someone with different experiences.

Evening: Reflect on how being open changed your perspective.

Classroom Activity: Write about a time you learned from someone unexpected.

Minds are like parachutes, they only function when open. – Thomas Dewar

Day 51

Flexibility in the Face of Change

Morning: Take three deep breaths and set the intention to be flexible today.

Afternoon: Do something slightly different from your usual routine.

Evening: Write about one unexpected moment today that helped you grow.

Classroom Activity: Write about a famous person who turned adversity into success.

The measure of intelligence is the ability to change. – Albert Einstein

Day 52

Curiosity in Times of Change

Morning: Repeat the affirmation: "I embrace change as an opportunity to grow."

Afternoon: Identify one area in your life where change is happening and view it with curiosity.

Evening: Reflect on a recent change and one positive outcome from it.

Classroom Activity: Discuss a time when a change led to unexpected benefits.

It is not the strongest of the species that survives, nor the most intelligent, but the one most responsive to change. – Charles Darwin

Day 53

Navigating Shifts with Confidence

Morning: Say: "I trust myself to handle whatever comes my way."

Afternoon: Observe your reactions when plans change and try to stay open.

Evening: Journal about a time you handled a shift well.

Classroom Activity: Practice mindfulness by adapting to a surprise classroom exercise.

Change your thoughts, and you change your world. – Norman Vincent Peale

Day 54

Taking Inspired Action

Morning: Set the intention: "I grow stronger through change."

Afternoon: Think about a current transition and list three positives about it.

Evening: Reflect on the most significant lesson change you have learned this week.

Classroom Activity: Create a "change resilience" action plan for a future challenge.

When we are no longer able to change a situation, we are challenged to change ourselves. – Viktor Frankl

Day 55

Adapting and Winning

Morning: Repeat: "I am resilient, adaptable, and strong."

Afternoon: Challenge yourself to remain calm during a minor inconvenience.

Evening: Note a way you handled change better than before.

Classroom Activity: Role-play how to handle unexpected difficulties.

Adaptability is about the decisive difference between adapting to cope and adapting to win. – *Max McKeown*

Day 56

Welcome New Experiences

Morning: Visualize yourself confidently handling an unexpected situation.

Afternoon: Try to welcome something new today instead of resisting it.

Evening: Reflect on a small success in adapting to something different.

Classroom Activity: Discuss how historical events shaped progress through change.

The art of life lies in a constant readjustment to our surroundings."– Kakuzo Okakura

Day 57

Taking Action Toward Goals

Morning: Say: "I trust the process of change in my life."

Afternoon: Take note of how your mindset influences your response to change.

Evening: Write down one action step to embrace future changes with confidence.

Classroom Activity: Share personal stories of change and how they led to growth.

Change begins at the end of your comfort zone. – Roy T. Bennett

Day 58

Progress in Small Steps

Morning: Close your eyes and visualize yourself successfully reaching a personal goal.

Afternoon: Break down a big goal into smaller, manageable steps and take one action toward it.

Evening: Write about how effort matters more than perfection.

Classroom Activity: Brainstorm different types of goals (academic, personal, physical) and discuss strategies to achieve them.

You don't have to see the whole staircase, take the first step. – Martin Luther King Jr.

Day 59

Persistence Drives Success

Morning: Set an intention: "I am capable of reaching my dreams."

Afternoon: Do one task, however small, that moves you closer to a long-term goal.

Evening: Reflect on how persistence plays a role in achieving success.

Classroom Activity: Each student writes one goal and an action step to take this week.

Small deeds done are better than great deeds planned. – Peter Marshall

Day 60

Reflecting on Progress and Obstacles

Morning: Picture yourself confidently overcoming an obstacle on your journey.

Afternoon: Seek advice or inspiration from someone who has achieved a goal similar to yours.

Evening: List three things you did today that brought you closer to success.

Classroom Activity: Group discussion: What are common obstacles to success, and how can we overcome them?

Obstacles are those frightful things you see when you take your eyes off your goal. – Henry Ford

Day 61

Staying Focused on the Goal

Morning: Repeat: "Every small step I take is bringing me closer to my dream."

Afternoon: Challenge yourself to stay focused for 15 minutes, avoiding distractions while working towards a goal.

Evening: Reflect on what motivated you most today and why.

Classroom Activity: Students create a visual "goal board" with images and words representing their aspirations.

The future depends on what you do today. – Mahatma Gandhi

Day 62

Celebrating Progress

Morning: Take a few moments to visualize the joy of reaching a milestone.

Afternoon: Commit to showing up for yourself by completing one task that aligns with your goal.

Evening: Write about how it feels to make progress, even if it's small.

Classroom Activity: Share stories of historical figures who overcame setbacks to achieve great things.

Success is the sum of small efforts, repeated day in and day out. – Robert Collier

Day 63

Cultivating Consistency and Confidence

Morning: Affirm: "I am capable, determined, and moving forward."

Afternoon: Identify one habit you can improve to help you stay consistent.

Evening: Celebrate your progress so far by writing a letter to your future self.

Classroom Activity: Create a class-wide goal and work together to take the first step toward achieving it.

Dream big. Start small. Act now. – Robin Sharma

Day 64

Stepping Outside Your Comfort Zone

Morning: Visualize yourself achieving your biggest goal with confidence.

Afternoon: Take one bold action today that pushes you out of your comfort zone.

Evening: Write about how resilience has helped you stay committed to your aspirations.

Classroom Activity: Students pair up and share one long-term goal, brainstorming creative ways to stay motivated.

Believe in yourself, for within you lies the strength to overcome any obstacle. – Kim Groshek

Day 65

Embracing Growth Through Change

Morning: Embrace uncertainty as an opportunity for growth.

Afternoon: Take one small action towards a goal despite uncertainty.

Evening: Journal how embracing change impacted your mindset today.

Classroom Activity: Students share a change they initially feared but later appreciated.

The secret of change is to focus all of your energy not on fighting the old but on building the new. – Socrates

Day 66

Shifting Your Perspective on Change

Morning: Identify an area in life where you're resisting change.

Afternoon: Challenge yourself to see this change differently.

Evening: Reflect on what flexibility means to you.

Classroom Activity: Discussion on adaptability in the face of uncertainty.

Progress is impossible without change, and those who cannot change their minds cannot change anything. – George Bernard Shaw

Day 67

Finding Gratitude in Change

Morning: Start your day with a gratitude list focused on changes.

Afternoon: Try a new approach to an everyday task.

Evening: Journal about an unexpected change and how it turned out well.

Classroom Activity: Debate: "Change is always good. Agree or disagree?"

Change is the only constant in life. – Heraclitus

Day 68

Learning from Life's Transitions

Morning: Set a goal to embrace one new experience today.

Afternoon: Take a moment to acknowledge the lessons from past changes.

Evening: Write about a change that shaped who you are today.

Classroom Activity: Create a vision board of positive changes for the future.

Growth and comfort do not coexist. – Ginni Rometty

Day 69

Welcoming Change with an Open Mind

Morning: Repeat, "I welcome change as an opportunity to grow."

Afternoon: Seek out and appreciate an unexpected change.

Evening: Reflect on how your mindset towards change has evolved.

Classroom Activity: Discuss ways to make peace with change.

Your life does not get better by chance, it gets better by change. – Jim Rohn

Day 70

New Possibilities Through Change

Morning: Recognize that every change leads to new possibilities.

Afternoon: Observe how you naturally respond to transitions.

Evening: Write down what excites you about the future.

Classroom Activity: Write a letter to your future self about embracing change.

Be the change that you wish to see in the world. – Mahatma Gandhi

Day 71

Celebrating Personal Growth and Fresh Beginnings

Morning: Set an intention to welcome new beginnings.

Afternoon: Take a moment to celebrate your personal growth this month.

Evening: Reflect on how pausing helped you embrace change.

Classroom Activity: Discuss personal takeaways from the month's exercises.

Every moment is a fresh beginning. – T.S. Eliot

Day 72

Living with Passion and Purpose

Morning: Identify one passion that brings you joy.

Noon: Take a moment to visualize how your actions align with your purpose.

Evening: Reflect on a small way you lived with purpose today.

Classroom Activity: Passion Project Brainstorm – Students explore what excites them.

The meaning of life is to find your gift. The purpose of life is to give it away. – Pablo Picasso

Day 73

Redefining Success and Fulfillment

Morning: Reflect on what success means to you beyond material wealth.

Noon: Take a break to recognize a moment of fulfillment today.

Evening: Write about how aligning with your values enhances your life.

Classroom Activity: Values Exploration – Identify personal values and how they shape decisions.

Success is not the key to happiness. Happiness is the key to success. – Albert Schweitzer

Day 74

The Power of Intentional Living

Morning: Affirm: "I am creating a meaningful and fulfilling life."

Noon: Take note of how you express your purpose in small daily actions.

Evening: Reflect on how living with intention affects your well-being.

Classroom Activity: Vision Board Creation – Illustrate personal goals and dreams.

Don't ask what the world needs. Ask what makes you come alive and go do it. – Howard Thurman.

Day 75

Taking Purposeful Action

Morning: Identify one action you can take to step closer to your purpose.

Noon: Pause to express gratitude for meaningful moments.

Evening: Reflect on how your purpose-driven actions impacted your day.

Classroom Activity: Purpose-Driven Challenge – Set small daily goals aligned with personal values.

Live as if you were to die tomorrow. Learn as if you were to live forever. – Mahatma Gandhi

Day 76

Reflection on Purpose and Meaning

Morning: Meditate on how purpose influences happiness.

Noon: Do something that profoundly fulfills you.

Evening: Journal about moments of purpose from the past month.

Act as if what you do makes a difference. It does. – William James.

Today has been about cultivating self-compassion, resilience, and purpose. Let me know if you need any refinements!

Day 77

Overcoming Self-Doubt and Building Confidence

Morning: Set a mantra: "I am capable and strong."

Noon: Recall a past challenge you overcame.

Evening: Reflect on one thing you learned today.

Classroom Activity: Confidence Collage – Create a visual board of strengths and accomplishments.

Doubt kills more dreams than failure ever will. – Suzy Kassem

Day 78

Strengthening Self-Belief

Morning: Practice power posing for 2 minutes.

Noon: Replace one negative thought with a positive affirmation.

Evening: Write down a time when you proved yourself wrong.

Classroom Activity: Positive Self-Talk – Discuss the impact of self-belief.

Believe you can, and you're halfway there. – Theodore Roosevelt

Day 79

Embracing Imperfection and Growth

Morning: Set an intention to embrace imperfections.

Noon: Take a mindful pause to acknowledge progress, not just results.

Evening: Identify a moment where you overcame a fear.

Classroom Activity: Growth Mindset Discussion – Share stories of learning from mistakes.

Perfection is the enemy of progress. – Winston Churchill

Day 80

Embracing Your Strengths

Morning: Name three personal strengths.

Noon: Recall a compliment you received and fully accept it.

Evening: Reflect on how your strengths supported you today.

Classroom Activity: Strengths Inventory – Students identify their top three strengths.

Strength doesn't come from what you can do. It comes from overcoming things you thought you couldn't. – Rikki Rogers

Day 81

Stepping Out of Your Comfort Zone

Morning: Write down one way you will step out of your comfort zone today.

Noon: Take a short break to do something that excites you.

Evening: Celebrate the courage it took to try something new.

Classroom Activity: Comfort Zone Challenge – Encourage students to do something new and reflect on it.

Everything you've ever wanted is on the other side of fear. – George Addair

Day 82

Building Confidence Through Reflection

Morning: Meditate on your past successes.

Noon: Engage in a self-care practice.

Evening: Write a letter to your future confident self.

Today: Plan three small ways to build confidence in the next week.

Confidence comes from discipline and training. – Robert Kiyosaki

Day 83

Cultivating a Growth Mindset

Morning: Repeat a positive affirmation about learning.

Afternoon: Identify a small mistake and reframe it as a learning opportunity.

Evening: Journal one success from today, no matter how small.

Classroom Activity: Write one thing you learned today and share with a partner.

Success is not final; failure is not fatal; it is the courage to continue that counts. – Winston Churchill

Day 84

Embracing Challenges for Growth

Morning: Take five deep breaths and set an intention for growth.

Afternoon: Try something new outside your comfort zone.

Evening: Reflect on a challenge and what it taught you.

Classroom Activity: Students discuss that they struggled but kept going one time.

Challenges are what make life interesting, and overcoming them is what makes life meaningful. – Joshua J. Marine

Day 85

Focusing on the Journey, Not Just the Outcome

Morning: List three qualities you admire in yourself.

Afternoon: Focus on the process of learning rather than results.

Evening: Write about how you responded to a challenge today.

Classroom Activity: Draw or write about a goal you want to achieve.

If you find a path with no obstacles, it probably doesn't lead anywhere. – Frank A. Clark

Day 86

Harnessing Persistence and Effort

Morning: Visualize yourself succeeding in a personal challenge.

Afternoon: Share a piece of knowledge with a friend.

Evening: Reflect on how effort and persistence shaped your day.

Classroom Activity: Students write letters to their future selves about what they hope to accomplish.

Do not be embarrassed by your failures, learn from them and start again. – Richard Branson

Day 87

Strengthening Resilience and Capability

Morning: Start the day by saying, "I am capable and resilient."

Afternoon: Identify one obstacle and brainstorm ways to overcome it.

Evening: Write about one improvement you noticed today.

Classroom Activity: Pair up and give each other one piece of positive feedback.

Believe you can, and you're halfway there. – Theodore Roosevelt

Day 88

Overcoming Limiting Beliefs

Morning: Identify one limiting belief and write its opposite.

Afternoon: Think of a time you proved a doubt wrong.

Evening: Reflect on what new belief you want to adopt.

Classroom Activity: Group discussion on self-imposed limitations and how to challenge them.

Your only limit is your mind.— Kim Groshek

Day 89

Proving Your Inner Strength

Morning: Say aloud, "I am limitless and capable."

Afternoon: Try a task you've been avoiding.

Evening: List three things you did today that proved your strength.

Classroom Activity: Role-play overcoming a fear or challenge.

Whether you think you can or you think you can't—you're right. – Henry Ford

Day 90

Breaking Free from Fear

Morning: Write down a fear and a reason why it's not true.

Afternoon: Tackle a small step toward overcoming a fear.

Evening: Journal about how it felt to push past a limiting belief.

Classroom Activity: Create a positive mantra to replace a common fear.

Doubt kills more dreams than failure ever will. – Suzy Kassem

Day 91

Learning from Setbacks: Embrace Failure as a Stepping Stone

Morning: Reflect on how you react to setbacks.

Afternoon: Find an opportunity in a past failure.

Evening: Write down one thing you learned today that surprised you.

Classroom Activity: Discuss a time when failure led to success.

Failure is simply the opportunity to begin again, this time more intelligently. – Henry Ford

Day 92

The Power of Open-Mindedness Learning from New Perspectives

Morning: Set an intention to stay open-minded today.

Afternoon: Seek advice from someone with different experiences.

Evening: Reflect on how being open changed your perspective.

Classroom Activity: Write about a time you learned from someone unexpected.

Minds are like parachutes, they only function when open. – Thomas Dewar

Day 93

Embracing Change & Resilience

Morning: Repeat the affirmation: "I embrace change as an opportunity to grow."

Afternoon: Identify one area in your life where change is happening and view it with curiosity.

Evening: Reflect on a recent change and one positive outcome from it.

Classroom Activity: Discuss a time when a change led to unexpected benefits.

It is not the strongest of the species that survives, nor the most intelligent, but the one most responsive to change. – Charles Darwin

Day 94

Flexibility & Growth
Navigating Change with Ease

Morning: Take 3 deep breaths and set the intention to be flexible today.

Afternoon: Do something slightly different from your usual routine.

Evening: Write about one unexpected moment today that helped you grow.

Classroom Activity: Write about a famous person who turned adversity into success.

The measure of intelligence is the ability to change. – Albert Einstein

Day 95

Trusting Yourself in Times of Change
Building Confidence

Morning: Say: "I trust myself to handle whatever comes my way."

Afternoon: Observe your reactions when plans change and try to stay open.

Evening: Journal about a time you handled a shift well.

Classroom Activity: Practice mindfulness by adapting to a surprise classroom exercise.

Change your thoughts, and you change your world. – Norman Vincent Peale

Day 96

Growing Through Change

Morning: Set the intention: "I grow stronger through change."

Afternoon: Think about a current transition and list three positives about it.

Evening: Reflect on the biggest lesson change has taught you this week.

Classroom Activity: Create a "change resilience" action plan for a future challenge.

When we are no longer able to change a situation, we are challenged to change ourselves. – Viktor Frankl

Day 97

Resilience in Action: Adapting to Life's Challenges

Morning: Repeat: "I am resilient, adaptable, and strong."

Afternoon: Challenge yourself to remain calm during a minor inconvenience.

Evening: Note a way you handled change better than before.

Classroom Activity: Role-play how to handle unexpected difficulties.

Adaptability is the decisive shift from merely coping to truly thriving. – Kim Groshek

Day 98

Embracing New Experiences
Welcoming the Unexpected

Morning: Visualize yourself confidently handling an unexpected situation.

Afternoon: Try to welcome something new today instead of resisting it.

Evening: Reflect on a small success in adapting to something different.

Classroom Activity: Discuss how historical events shaped progress through change.

The art of life lies in a constant readjustment to our surroundings. – Kakuzo Okakura

Day 99

The Confidence to Change
Trusting the Process

Morning: Say: "I trust the process of change in my life."

Afternoon: Take note of how your mindset influences your response to change.

Evening: Write down one action step to embrace future changes with confidence.

Classroom Activity: Share personal stories of change and how they led to growth.

Change begins at the end of your comfort zone. – Roy T. Bennett

Day 100

Moving Forward with Purpose

Morning: Close your eyes and visualize yourself successfully reaching a personal goal.

Afternoon: Break down a big goal into smaller, manageable steps and take one action toward it.

Evening: Write about how effort matters more than perfection.

Classroom Activity: Brainstorm different types of goals (academic, personal, physical) and discuss strategies to achieve them.

You don't need to see the entire staircase—trust your dynamic spirit and take that first bold step. – Kim Groshek

Day 101

Taking Action Toward Goals

Morning: Set an intention: "I am capable of reaching my dreams."

Afternoon: Do one task, however small, that moves you closer to a long-term goal.

Evening: Reflect on how persistence plays a role in achieving success.

Classroom Activity: Each student writes one goal and an action step to take this week.

Small deeds done are better than great deeds planned. – Peter Marshall

Day 102

Overcoming Obstacles to Success

Morning: Picture yourself confidently overcoming an obstacle on your journey.

Afternoon: Seek advice or inspiration from someone who has achieved a goal similar to yours.

Evening: List three things you did today that brought you closer to success.

Classroom Activity: Group discussion: What are common obstacles to success, and how can we overcome them?

Obstacles are those frightful things you see when you take your eyes off your goal. – Henry Ford

Day 103

Small Steps, Big Dreams

Morning: Repeat: "Every small step I take is bringing me closer to my dream."

Afternoon: Challenge yourself to stay focused and avoid distractions for 15 minutes while working toward a goal.

Evening: Reflect on what motivated you most today and why.

Classroom Activity: Students create a visual "goal board" with images and words representing their aspirations.

The future depends on what you do today. – Mahatma Gandhi

Day 104

Celebrating Small Wins

Morning: Take a few moments to visualize the joy of reaching a milestone.

Afternoon: Commit to showing up for yourself by completing one task that aligns with your goal.

Evening: Write about how it feels to make progress, even if it's small.

Classroom Activity: Share stories of historical figures who overcame setbacks to achieve great things.

Success is the sum of small efforts, repeated day in and day out. – Robert Collier

Day 105

Building Consistency
One Habit at a Time

Morning: Affirm: "I am capable, determined, and moving forward."

Afternoon: Identify one habit you can improve to help you stay consistent.

Evening: Celebrate your progress so far by writing a letter to your future self.

Classroom Activity: Create a class-wide goal and work together to take the first step toward achieving it.

Dream big. Start small. Act now. – Robin Sharma

Day 106

The Power of Resilience

Morning: Visualize yourself achieving your biggest goal with confidence.

Afternoon: Take one bold action today that pushes you out of your comfort zone.

Evening: Write about how resilience has helped you stay committed to your aspirations.

Classroom Activity: Students pair up and share one long-term goal, brainstorming creative ways to stay motivated.

Resilience is the strength to keep moving forward, even when the path seems challenging—trust in your inner power. – Kim Groshek

Day 107

Growth in Change

Morning: Embrace uncertainty as an opportunity for growth.

Afternoon: Take one small action towards a goal despite uncertainty.

Evening: Journal how embracing change impacted your mindset today.

Classroom Activity: Students share a change they initially feared but later appreciated.

The secret of change is to focus all of your energy not on fighting the old but on building the new. – Socrates

Day 108

Flexibility
Adapting to Life's Shifts

Morning: Identify an area in life where you're resisting change.

Afternoon: Challenge yourself to see this change differently.

Evening: Reflect on what flexibility means to you.

Classroom Activity: Discussion on adaptability in the face of uncertainty.

Progress is impossible without change, and those who cannot change their minds cannot change anything. – George Bernard Shaw

Day 109

Embracing Growth Through Change

Morning: Start your day with a gratitude list focused on changes.

Afternoon: Try a new approach to an everyday task.

Evening: Journal about an unexpected change and how it turned out well.

Classroom Activity: Debate: "Change is always good. Agree or disagree?"

Change is the only constant in life. – Heraclitus

Day 110

Embracing Growth Through Change

Morning: Set a goal to embrace one new experience today.

Afternoon: Take a moment to acknowledge the lessons from past changes.

Evening: Write about a change that shaped who you are today.

Classroom Activity: Create a vision board of positive changes for the future.

Growth and comfort do not coexist. – Ginni Rometty

Day 111

Stepping into New Experiences

Morning: Repeat, "I welcome change as an opportunity to grow."

Afternoon: Seek out and appreciate an unexpected change.

Evening: Reflect on how your mindset towards change has evolved.

Classroom Activity: Discuss ways to make peace with change.

Your life does not get better by chance; it gets better through change. – Jim Rohn

Day 112

Welcome Change As Growth

Morning: Recognize that every change leads to new possibilities.

Afternoon: Observe how you naturally respond to transitions.

Evening: Write down what excites you about the future.

Classroom Activity: Write a letter to your future self about embracing change.

Be the change that you wish to see in the world. – Mahatma Gandhi

Day 113

Reflecting on Growth
Personal Takeaways

Morning: Set an intention to welcome new beginnings.

Afternoon: Take a moment to celebrate your personal growth this month.

Evening: Reflect on how pausing helped you embrace change.

Classroom Activity: Discuss personal takeaways from the month's exercises.

Every moment is a fresh beginning. – T.S. Eliot

Day 114

Awareness of the Present Moment

Morning: Practice mindful breathing for five minutes.

Noon: Take a mindful walk, observing surroundings without judgment.

Evening: Reflect on three things you noticed today that you usually overlook.

Classroom Activity: Sensory Awareness Challenge – Describe an object using all five senses.

Transformation's magic unfolds in the present; pausing empowers awareness, deepens connection, and fuels dynamic growth.– Kim Groshek

Day 115

Deepening Self-Awareness

Morning: Set a mindful intention for the day.

Noon: Pause and check in with your emotions—how do you feel?

Evening: Journal about one moment where you felt fully present.

Classroom Activity: Emotion Mapping – Identify emotions experienced throughout the day.

Self-awareness arises in pauses, reconnecting us with our true essence.– Kim Groshek

Day 116

Mindful Communication

Morning: Practice gratitude by sending a kind message to someone.

Noon: Engage in an active listening exercise—fully focus on a conversation.

Evening: Reflect on one meaningful interaction you had today.

Classroom Activity: Pair discussions—share something new about yourself with a classmate.

Mindful communication starts with being present and listening deeply with our hearts. Genuine connection flourishes through intention, empathy, and shared vulnerability. – Kim Groshek

Day 117

Mindful Goal Setting

Morning: Begin the day by setting one mindful goal.

Noon: Perform an act of kindness without expectation.

Evening: Reflect on how intentional living shaped your day.

Classroom Activity: Create a personal manifesto for mindful living.

Wisdom from mindful leaders on presence and awareness. – Kim Groshek.

Day 118

Pausing to Manage Stress Effectively

Morning: Take three deep breaths and set an intention for a calm and productive day.

Afternoon: Step away from screens and take a short walk or stretch.

Evening: Reflect on moments of stress and how you responded.

Classroom Practice: Discuss stress triggers and healthy coping strategies.

Almost everything will work again if you unplug it for a few minutes, including you. – Anne Lamott

Day 119

Gratitude and Mindfulness
Finding Calm

Morning: Write down three things you're grateful for.

Afternoon: Practice mindful breathing for one minute.

Evening: Journal about one thing that went well today.

Classroom Practice: Guided meditation session.

Tension is who you think you should be. Relaxation is who you are. – Chinese Proverb

Day 120

Stress Management Mastery

Morning: Visualize yourself handling stress with ease.

Afternoon: Take a hydration break and drink water mindfully.

Evening: Write about a stressor and one action you can take to ease it.

Classroom Practice: Create a personal stress-management plan.

A calm mind brings inner strength and self-confidence. – Dalai Lama

Day 121

Letting Go with Ease

Morning: Close your eyes, breathe deeply, and set an intention to release control.

Noon: Walk mindfully, silently affirming, "I let go of what no longer serves me."

Evening: Reflect on what you released and note one gratitude.

Classroom: Journal about surrendering control.

"*Letting go is powerful.*" – Kim Groshek.

Day 122

The Freedom of Release

Morning: Breathe deeply, releasing resistance. Affirm, "I trust the process of life."

Noon: Stretch mindfully, envisioning tension melting away.

Evening: Focus on a candle's flame, imagining worries dissolving. End with gratitude.

Classroom: Write what you're releasing and place it in a "letting go" box.

"Let go of thoughts that don't make you strong." – Karen Salmansohn

Day 123

Centering and Setting Intentions

Morning: Breathe deeply, center yourself, and set a clear intention. Visualize success. Affirm: *"I am focused and ready."*

Noon: Pause to reset. Reflect on progress and refocus. Affirm: *"I am calm and aligned."*

Evening: Reflect on achievements, note three gratitudes, and affirm growth.

Classroom: Practice 30 minutes of distraction-free focus, then reflect.

"Happiness is the key to success." – Albert Schweitzer.

Day 124

Aligning with Purpose

Morning Pause: Sit tall, align your spine, and focus on your breath. Choose a keyword like *Focus* or *Calm* to set your intention.

Noon Pause: Close your eyes, breathe deeply, and check in with your energy to stay grounded.

Evening Pause: Reflect on wins, express gratitude, and release tension.

Classroom Practice: Track time in 30-minute increments to reduce distractions.

"The secret of getting ahead is getting started." –
Mark Twain

Day 125

Intentional Progress

Morning Pause: Breathe mindfully, set a clear goal, and break it into steps.

Noon Pause: Reset, clear your mind, and refocus on priorities.

Evening Pause: Reflect on wins, express gratitude, and breathe deeply for calm.

Classroom Practice: Try a 25-minute focus session, then compare productivity with distractions.

Don't watch the clock; do what it does. Keep going. – Sam Levenson

Day 126

Embrace Focus and Clarity

Morning Pause: Find a quiet space, breathe deeply, and affirm: *"Today, I focus on what matters most."* Visualize success.

Noon Pause: Breathe deeply, eliminate distractions, refocus, and choose two actions to realign with goals.

Evening Pause: Reflect, express gratitude, and release tension.

Classroom Practice: Work distraction-free for 30 minutes, then reflect.

Success finds those who focus on the journey, not the destination. – Kim Groshek

Day 127

Clarity and Action

Morning Pause: Sit tall, breathe deeply, visualize your goals, set an achievable task, and affirm: *"I am clear and ready."*

Noon Pause: Breathe deeply, identify distractions, list next steps, and affirm focus on priorities.

Evening Pause: Reflect with gratitude, note two wins, and breathe deeply.

Classroom Practice: Track time and categorize activities for better focus.

Don't wait. The time will never be just right. – Napoleon Hill

Day 128

The Power of Presence in Leadership

Morning Pause: Inhale, hold, and exhale for four counts. Repeat for three minutes.

Noon Pause: Lead with presence—listen actively and make others feel valued.

Evening Pause: Reflect on a moment of true presence. Write its impact.

Classroom Practice: Students write down a time they were fully present in conversation.

Leadership isn't control—it's caring for those you're entrusted to uplift. – Kim Groshek.

Day 129

The Impact of Focused Leadership

Morning Pause: Ground yourself, close your eyes, and choose one task to give your full attention. Set an intention to stay focused and intentional.

Noon Pause: Breathe deeply, silence distractions, and visualize completing your task.

Evening Pause: Reflect on a task completed with full attention. How did it impact your leadership?

Classroom Practice: Identify a distraction and stay focused on one task for 15 minutes.

"The successful warrior is the average man, with laser-like focus." – Bruce Lee

Day 130

Empowering Through Presence

Morning Pause: Breathe deeply, sit comfortably, and set an intention to empower through presence.

Noon Pause: Reflect on leadership: How can your presence inspire growth?

Evening Pause: Recall when your presence made a difference. Write how you empowered someone.

Classroom Practice: Practice active listening—one speaks while the other listens fully, without interruptions.

Leadership is about uplifting others, not being the best. – Kim Groshek

Day 131

Leading with Energy and Focus

Morning Pause: Breathe deeply, visualize a productive day, and choose one action to boost leadership energy.

Noon Pause: Check in with your focus and recharge through a mindful break.

Evening Pause: Reflect on your energy. What helped or hindered focus? Write key insights.

Classroom Practice: Identify energy drains and boosts, creating strategies for sustainability.

"Energy is the key to high performance. It's the foundation of leadership." – Tony Schwartz

Day 132

The Power of Active Listening

Morning Pause: Breathe deeply and set an intention to listen with understanding, not just response.

Noon Pause: Reflect on a conversation. How can you improve your listening? Visualize.

Evening Pause: Reflect on active listening. How did it affect the conversation? Write it down.

Classroom Practice: Practice reflective listening—one speaks, and the other summarizes to confirm understanding.

"The most important thing in communication is hearing what isn't said." – Peter Drucker.

Day 133

Authenticity in Leadership

Morning Pause: Breathe deeply and set an intention to lead authentically. Ask, "How can I be my true self today?"

Noon Pause: Reflect on inauthentic moments and reframe them, embracing vulnerability and commitment to authenticity.

Evening Pause: Recall a moment of authenticity. Write down its impact.

Classroom Practice: Role-play authentic vs. inauthentic leadership scenarios in pairs.

"The best way to find yourself is to lose yourself in the service of others." – Mahatma Gandhi.

Day 134

Cultivating Presence and Calm

Morning Pause: Close your eyes, breathe deeply, and set an intention to stay calm despite challenges.

Noon Pause: Take a deep breath and reflect on ways to stay calm in stress.

Evening Pause: Recall a challenging moment today. How did you stay present and calm, and what was the outcome?

Classroom Practice: Lead students in a 3-minute breathing exercise to enhance mindfulness.

Calmness is the cradle of power. – Josiah Gilbert Holland.

Day 135

Building Connection Through Presence

Morning Pause: Set an intention to create meaningful connections today by being fully present with others.

Noon Pause: Reflect on interactions. Choose one person to engage with more deeply today.

Evening Pause: Reflect on a meaningful connection. How did presence impact the relationship?

Classroom Practice: Ask students to write about a time they felt deeply connected to someone.

The richest build networks; others focus on finding work. – Kim Groshek

Day 136

Deepening Conversations

Morning Pause: Set an intention to actively listen and stay open to others' perspectives.

Noon Pause: Reflect on conversations—were they meaningful? Guide future talks for depth.

Evening Pause: Recall a vulnerable conversation. How did it strengthen your connection?

Classroom Practice: Pair students with deep listening and open-ended questions. Discuss the experience.

The most important thing in communication is hearing what isn't said.– Peter Drucker

Day 137

Listening to Understand

Morning Pause: Set an intention to listen with understanding, focusing on the emotions and intentions behind the words.

Noon Pause: Reflect on a conversation—did you listen to understand or prepare your response? How can you deepen your listening?

Evening Pause: Recall a conversation where you truly listened. How did it improve your connection?

Classroom Practice: Share experiences in pairs while the other listens and reflects on feelings."

When people talk, listen completely. Most people never listen. – Ernest Hemingway.

Day 138

The Power of Silence in Connection

Morning Pause: Breathe deeply and reflect on the power of silence. Set an intention to use silence as a tool for connection today, allowing others to speak and be heard.

Noon Pause: Reflect on how silence strengthens connection. Can it help others open up or feel understood?

Evening Pause: Recall a conversation where silence enhanced your connection.

Classroom Practice: Practice a "silent conversation" exercise to deepen listening.

"Silence is a source of great strength." – Lao Tzu

Day 139

Vulnerability and Trust

Morning: Reflect on how vulnerability strengthens relationships. Set an intention to be open.

Noon: Identify a moment to share more of yourself. Visualize deeper connection.

Evening: Reflect on when you showed vulnerability today. How did it impact others?

Classroom: Students journal about a vulnerable moment that deepened a connection.

"Vulnerability is not winning or losing; it's having the courage to show up and be seen." – Brené Brown.

Day 140

Building Rapport with Empathy

Morning: Breathe deeply and set an intention to understand others with empathy.

Noon: Reflect on interactions—how can you show more empathy? Choose one person.

Evening: Recall an empathetic moment today. How did it strengthen your connection?

Classroom: Students share struggles with a partner, responding with empathy, not advice.

"*Leadership is caring for those you serve.*" – Kim Groshek.

Day 141

Reflecting on Connection

Morning: Breathe deeply and set an intention to create meaningful connections today.

Noon: Assess your interactions. Which relationships need more attention?

Evening: Recall a deep connection today. How did it feel? What did you learn?

Classroom: Students choose one connection to deepen and plan to show up authentically.

"True networking thrives on generosity, not greed." – Keith Ferrazzi.

Day 142

Leading with Empathy

Morning Pause: Focus on your breath and set an intention to lead with empathy, considering how others might feel today.

Noon Pause: Reflect on how empathy has influenced your leadership so far. What can you do to lead with more compassion?

Evening Pause: Recall a moment where you led with empathy. How did it impact the relationship or outcome?

Classroom Practice: Have students reflect on an empathetic leader and write about their actions.

To lead people, walk beside them. – Lao Tzu

Day 143

Daily Pause for Self-Compassion:

Morning: Breathe deeply and affirm, "I lead with kindness, starting with myself."

Noon: Reflect on a mistake. Replace self-criticism with compassion. What advice would you give a friend?

Evening Pause: Reflect on how self-compassion shaped your leadership today.

Classroom Practice: Have students write a letter offering themselves compassion for a recent challenge.

Lead yourself with kindness and compassion first—only then can you lead others. – Kim Groshek

Day 144

Leading with Mindful Presence

Morning: Breathe deeply and set an intention to be fully present in conversations today.

Noon: Reflect on your leadership interactions. Were you present? How can you improve?

Evening: Recall one conversation where you were fully present. What was the outcome?

Classroom: Students practice "mindful listening," summarizing without interruption.

Wherever you are, be all there. – Jim Elliot

Day 145

Servant Leadership and Putting Others First

Morning Pause: Set an intention to serve others today through support or guidance.

Noon Pause: Reflect on an act of service today. How did it impact you and others?

Evening Pause: Journal one way to lead with service and humility tomorrow.

Classroom Practice: Have students brainstorm small acts of service to commit to for the next day.

The best way to find yourself is to lose yourself in the service of others. – Mahatma Gandhi.

Day 146

Cultivating Emotional Intelligence in Leadership

Morning Pause: Reflect on your emotions and set an intention for self-awareness in leadership.

Noon Pause: Consider an emotional interaction today. How did you respond? How can you improve next time?

Evening Pause: Journal about an intense emotion felt today and its impact on your leadership.

Classroom Practice: Teach emotional intelligence components and have students identify one area for improvement.

Leadership is about taking care of those in your charge. – Simon Sinek.

Day 147

Leading with Courage and Vulnerability

Morning Pause: Set an intention to lead with courage, embracing discomfort.

Noon Pause: Reflect on a moment today when you embraced courage. How did it shape the situation?

Evening Pause: Journal about a lesson learned from showing courage.

Classroom Practice: Have students share a courageous moment and its impact.

"Courage begins with showing up and being seen." – Brené Brown.

Day 148

Mindfulness in Leadership Decision-Making

Morning: Clear your mind and set an intention to make thoughtful, mindful decisions today.

Noon: Reflect on a decision made today. Was it rushed or mindful? What did you learn?

Evening: Consider a leadership decision for tomorrow. How can you approach it wisely?

Classroom: Students role-play scenarios requiring mindful decision-making.

"The best leaders align their head, heart, and gut in decision-making." – Kim Groshek

Day 149

Defining Your Leadership Values

Morning: Reflect on the values guiding your leadership. Set an intention to lead with integrity.

Noon: Write your top three leadership values. Are your actions aligning with them?

Evening: Journal one example where you upheld your values today.

Classroom: Students list their top five values and discuss how they guide decisions.

Your values guide you; follow them to lead authentically. – Kim Groshek

Day 150

Creating a Leadership Mission Statement

Morning Pause: Set an intention to reflect on your leadership mission today.

Noon Pause: Write a short mission statement that captures your leadership purpose.

Evening Pause: Review your mission statement. Does it align with how you lead?

Classroom Practice: Have students write their own leadership mission statements and share them with a partner.

"A leader knows the way, goes the way, and shows the way." – John C. Maxwell

Day 151

Lifelong Learning in Leadership

Morning Pause: Set an intention to embrace curiosity and a willingness to learn today.

Noon Pause: Reflect on something new you've learned today and how it can enhance your leadership.

Evening Pause: Journal about a skill or topic you want to explore further.

Classroom Practice: Students set a learning goal and research a leader who embodies continuous learning.

True listening is about understanding, not just waiting to reply.– Kim Groshek

Day 152

The Foundation of Leadership is Presence

Morning Pause: Take a deep breath and affirm, "I am fully present today."

Noon Pause: Reflect on a moment when you were truly present.

Evening Pause: Journal about how your presence influenced your leadership today.

Classroom Practice: Discuss how presence can enhance leadership effectiveness.

"Leadership is about making others better as a result of your presence." – Sheryl Sandberg

Day 153

Active Listening as a Leadership Skill

Morning Pause: Set an intention to listen fully without distractions today.

Noon Pause: Reflect on a conversation where you practiced active listening.

Evening Pause: Journal about how listening enhanced your connection with others.

Classroom Practice: Pair students for a mindful listening exercise.

Most people do not listen with the intent to understand; they listen with the intent to reply. – Stephen R. Covey

Day 154

Refining Your Leadership Vision

Morning Pause: Set an intention to reflect deeply on your leadership journey.

Noon Pause: Write down three key lessons you've learned this month.

Evening Pause: Journal about how you will continue to grow as a leader.

Classroom Practice: Have students present their leadership vision for the future.

The function of leadership is to produce more leaders, not more followers. – Ralph Nader

Day 155

Understanding Money Beliefs

Morning: Reframe a limiting money belief into a positive affirmation.

Afternoon: Journal about early money influences and identify one belief to release.

Evening: Visualize financial success, read an abundance quote, and note an insight.

Classroom: Reflect on early money experiences and discuss their impact.

"The only limit to your impact is your imagination and commitment." – Tony Robbins.

Day 156

Building Healthy Financial Habits

Morning: Commit to mindful spending and track one financial decision.

Afternoon: Identify one expense to cut and reflect on needs vs. wants.

Evening: Review spending patterns and set a small financial goal.

Classroom: Plan a budget, balancing needs and wants.

"*Spend what is left after saving.*" – Warren Buffett.

Day 157

Expanding Your Imagination

Morning: Visualize a world without limits, exploring new possibilities and creative ideas.

Afternoon: Engage in a creative activity like doodling, brainstorming, or problem-solving.

Evening: Reflect on the most imaginative thought of the day and how to bring it to life.

Classroom: Create a story or drawing based on a random object.

"Imagination bridges what is and what could be— dare to cross it." – Kim Groshek.

Day 158

Investing in Growth

Morning: List three growth investments—learning, networking, or new experiences.

Afternoon: Identify a skill or course that fits your goals and plan the next step.

Evening: Reflect on how lifelong learning enriches your life and select a mentor or resource.

Classroom: Pitch a business idea addressing a real-world need.

An investment in knowledge pays the best interest.
– Benjamin Franklin.

Day 159

Giving & Gratitude for Wealth

Morning: Start your morning by listing three financial blessings and one way to give back.

Afternoon: Recall when generosity yielded unexpected rewards and send a note.

Evening: Donate, volunteer, or share resources while reflecting on giving's abundance.

Classroom: Discuss how generosity impacts personal and financial well-being.

No one has ever become poor by giving. – Anne Frank.

Day 160

Expanding Abundance Mindset

Morning: Meditate on wealth and set three financial goals for the next three months.

Afternoon: Study a successful person's approach to abundance and adopt one financial habit.

Evening: Reflect on your abundance and take a small step toward a big goal.

Classroom: Create a Financial Vision Board of abundance and success.

Success isn't measured by what you own but by who you become. – Kim Groshek

Day 161

Thinking Outside the Box

Morning Pause (5 min): Close your eyes, take deep breaths, and set an intention for creativity today.

Noon Pause (5-10 min): Brainstorm 10 creative ideas in 5 minutes. Let your imagination flow.

Evening Pause (3-5 min): Reflect: What idea excited you the most today?

Classroom Activity: Impossible Challenge – Solve a fun problem unconventionally.

Creativity is intelligence, and having fun. – Albert Einstein

Day 162

Creativity & Innovation

Morning Pause: Visualize yourself being innovative and open-minded.

Noon Pause: Choose one idea from yesterday and expand on it.

Evening Pause: Reflect: What did you notice when you allowed yourself to think differently?

Classroom Activity: Students work in pairs to come up with unique solutions to common problems.

The best way to predict the future is to create it. – Peter Drucker

Day 163

Overcoming Creative Blocks

Morning Pause: Breathe deeply and release tension. Say, "I am open to inspiration."

Noon Pause: Step away from work and go for a 10-minute walk. Let your mind wander.

Evening Pause: Reflect: What small moment of inspiration did you experience today

Classroom Activity: Creative Remix – Take an everyday object and find a new use for it.

Creativity takes courage. – Henri Matisse

Day 164

The Power of Play & Experimentation

Morning Pause: Smile and embrace the idea of play today.

Noon Pause: Try something new with no pressure to succeed.

Evening Pause: Reflect: What was fun or surprising about today?

Classroom Activity: Spontaneous Storytelling – Students create a group story, one line at a time.

Play is the highest form of research. – Albert Einstein

Day 165

Bringing Ideas to Life

Morning Pause: Visualize an idea you want to bring to life.

Noon Pause: Take the first step—no matter how small—toward making it real.

Evening Pause: Reflect: How did it feel to take action?

Classroom Activity: Mini Passion Project – Work on a creative project of choice.

Start where you are. Use what you have. Do what you can. – Arthur Ashe

Day 166

Strengthening Relationships Through Presence

Morning Pause: Set an intention to listen deeply today.

Noon Pause: Practice active listening in a conversation—focus entirely on the speaker.

Evening Pause: Reflect: How did being fully present impact your interactions

Classroom Activity: Deep Listening Exercise – Students pair up and practice mindful listening.

We have two ears and one mouth so that we can listen twice as much as we speak. – Epictetus

Day 167

Deepening Connections Through Mindful Communication

Morning: Express gratitude for the people in your life.

Noon: Pause before responding in conversations, allowing space to truly listen.

Evening: Reflect on how practicing presence has improved your relationships.

Classroom: Mindful Connection Circle – Share one thing you appreciated about someone today.

Connection is why we're here; it gives purpose and meaning to our lives. – Brené Brown

Day 168

The Art of Letting Go & Guided Meditation

Morning: Close your eyes, breathe deeply, and acknowledge any fear-based thoughts without judgment.

Noon: Write down one fear and reframe it into a possibility.

Evening: Reflect on how acknowledging your fear helped you today.

Classroom: Discuss common fears and strategies to shift perspectives.

Everything you want is on the other side of fear. – Jack Canfield

Day 169

Facing Fear with Courage

Morning Pause: Breathe deeply and observe any fear-based thoughts that arise.

Noon Pause: Identify one small action to challenge a limiting belief.

Evening Pause: Reflect: How did taking action shift your perspective?

Classroom Activity: Identify fears holding back creative expression and brainstorm ways to overcome them.

Do the thing you fear most, and the death of fear is certain. – Mark Twain

Day 170

Choosing Courage Over Fear

Morning Pause: Set an intention: "I choose courage over fear today."

Noon Pause: Visualize a positive outcome from overcoming a current fear.

Evening Pause: Reflect: What fears did you notice but not let control your actions

Classroom Activity: Write about a past fear you conquered and how it changed you.

Fear is a reaction. Courage is a decision. – Winston Churchill.

Day 171

Finding Strength in Overcoming Fear

Morning Pause: Focus on gratitude for something that once scared you but now empowers you.

Noon Pause: Take a mindful walk and observe how fear feels in your body.

Evening Pause: Reflect: What did your body teach you about fear today?

Classroom Activity: Partner exercise—students share how they overcame past fears.

He who has overcome his fears will truly be free. – Aristotle

Day 172

Building Confidence by Conquering Fear

Morning: Affirm: "I trust myself to handle any challenge that comes my way."

Noon: Identify a fear holding you back and take one small step toward overcoming it.

Evening: Reflect on what you learned from stepping outside your comfort zone.

Classroom: Fear Ladder Exercise – Rank fears and break them into actionable steps.

Courage is not the absence of fear but rather the judgment that something else is more important than fear. – Ambrose Redmoon

Day 173

Embracing Discomfort for Growth

Morning Pause: Deep breaths while repeating: "I release fear and embrace confidence."

Noon Pause: Try a new experience outside your comfort zone.

Evening Pause: Reflect: How did embracing discomfort help you grow today?

Classroom Activity: Guided visualization—imagine a future self who has overcome fear.

Fear is only as deep as the mind allows. –
Japanese Proverb

Day 174

Learning from Fear and Personal Growth

Morning Pause: Meditate on a past success where you overcame fear.

Noon Pause: Write down three reasons why you are capable of handling fear.

Evening Pause: Reflect: How does recognizing past successes build confidence

Classroom Activity: A group discussion on how fear has shaped personal growth.

What would life be if we had no courage to attempt anything? – Vincent Van Gogh

Day 175

Mindfulness Exercises to Build Confidence

Morning Pause: Breathe deeply and set an intention: "I am confident and capable."

Noon Pause: Practice a grounding exercise, focusing on your senses to stay present.

Evening Pause: Reflect: What moment today made you feel strong?

Classroom Activity: Mindful breathing exercises to enhance focus and self-assurance.

Confidence comes not from always being right but from not fearing to be wrong. – Peter T. McIntyre

Day 176

Mindfulness Exercises to Build Confidence

Morning Pause (5 min): Take three deep breaths and repeat: "I am strong, I am capable, I am confident."

Noon Pause (5-10 min): Identify an area where you feel self-doubt and reframe it into self-belief.

Evening Pause (3-5 min): Reflect: What small act of confidence did you practice today?

Classroom Activity: Discuss how shifting self-talk impacts performance and confidence.

Whether you think you can or you think you can't—you're right. – Henry Ford

Day 177

Embracing Self-Appreciation

Morning Pause: Set an intention to approach the day with curiosity instead of fear.

Noon Pause: Write down three things you like about yourself.

Evening Pause: Reflect: How did self-appreciation change your mindset today?

Classroom Activity: Mirror Exercise—students practice complimenting themselves.

Confidence comes not from always being right but from not fearing being wrong. – Peter T. McIntyre

Day 178

Stepping Into Courage

Morning Pause: Meditate on a moment when you felt truly powerful.

Noon Pause: Choose one thing you've been hesitant about and take a small action toward it.

Evening Pause: Reflect: How did stepping into action shift your energy today?

Classroom Activity: Role-play scenarios that require self-confidence.

Do one thing every day that scares you. – Eleanor Roosevelt

Day 179

Visualizing Success

Morning Pause: Repeat the affirmation: "I am learning, growing, and improving every day."

Noon Pause: Close your eyes and visualize yourself succeeding at something that scares you.

Evening Pause: Reflect: How did visualization impact your confidence today?

Classroom Activity: Vision Board—students create a confidence-building collage.

Believe you can, and you're halfway there. – Theodore Roosevelt

Day 180

Embodying Confidence

Morning Pause: Identify one thing you're proud of about yourself.

Noon Pause: Take a mindful walk and notice how confidence feels in your body.

Evening Pause: Reflect: What did your body language reveal about your confidence?

Classroom Activity: Posture & Presence—students practice confident body language.

To love oneself is the beginning of a lifelong romance. – Oscar Wilde

Day 181

Building Momentum for Success and Happiness

Morning Pause: Affirm: "I am worthy of success and happiness."

Noon Pause: Identify and celebrate a small win from the day.

Evening Pause: Reflect: How does celebrating progress build momentum?

Classroom Activity: Group celebration—students share small victories and encourage one another.

Success is liking yourself, liking what you do, and liking how you do it. – Maya Angelou

Day 182

Cultivating Confidence Through Pause

Morning Pause: Sit in stillness and focus on your breath, allowing confidence to flow through you.

Noon Pause: Write down a fear that no longer has power over you.

Evening Pause: Reflect: How does recognizing your growth strengthen confidence?

Classroom Activity: Journal Exercise—students write a letter to their past selves about overcoming fears.

Act as if what you do makes a difference. It does.– William James

Day 183

Taking Inspired Action Despite Fear

Morning Pause: Visualize yourself taking bold action today.

Noon Pause: Take one small courageous step toward a goal.

Evening Pause: Reflect: How did it feel to push past hesitation?

Classroom Activity: Group challenge—encourage students to step outside their comfort zone.

Do one thing every day that scares you. – Eleanor Roosevelt

Day 184

Taking Inspired Action Despite Fear

Morning Pause: Sit in stillness and focus on your breath, allowing confidence to flow through you.

Noon Pause: Write down a fear that no longer has power over you.

Evening Pause: Reflect: How does recognizing your growth strengthen confidence?

Classroom Activity: Journal Exercise—students write a letter to their past selves about overcoming fears.

You don't have to see the whole staircase. Just take the first step.– Martin Luther King Jr.

Day 185

Harnessing Confidence Through Reflection and Storytelling

Morning Pause: Visualize yourself confidently accomplishing something challenging today.

Noon Pause: Identify one past success that resulted from taking action and recall how it felt.

Evening Pause: Reflect: How does remembering past victories fuel future courage?

Classroom Activity: Storytelling—students share a time they took action despite fear.

Action is the foundational key to all success. – Pablo Picasso

Day 186

Embrace Fearlessness and Growth

Morning Pause: Repeat: "I am fearless in pursuit of my goals."

Noon Pause: Choose one thing outside your comfort zone and take a small step toward it.

Evening Pause: Reflect: What emotions did you experience before and after taking action?

Classroom Activity: Comfort Zone Challenge—students commit to a small, bold action.

Courage starts with showing up and letting ourselves be seen.– Brené Brown

Day 187

Tiny Habits That Increase Daily Joy

Morning Pause: Breathe deeply, smile, and set the intention to find joy in small moments today.

Noon Pause: Step outside, breathe deeply, and appreciate something beautiful. Stretch to release tension.

Evening Pause: Reflect on three joyful moments from today with gratitude.

Classroom Practice: Gratitude Jar – Write and share a joyful moment.

Daily Abundance Quote: *"Happiness is not something ready-made. It comes from your actions." — Dalai Lama.*

Day 188

A Daily Pause for Clarity and Confidence

Morning Pause: Take three deep breaths and embrace the mindset of "progress over perfection."

Noon Pause: Ask yourself, "What's the worst that could happen?" and write down a realistic outcome.

Evening Pause: Reflect: Did fear exaggerate the challenge in your mind? How did reality compare?

Classroom Activity: Worst-Case Scenario—Students challenge irrational fears by discussing realistic outcomes.

Use what you have, now.– Kim Groshek

Day 189

Embodying Growth: Small Steps & Bold Actions

Morning Pause: Meditate on the phrase "Every small step counts."

Noon Pause: Identify an inspiring role model and one trait they exhibit that you admire.

Evening Pause: Reflect: How can you embody that trait in your daily life?

Classroom Activity: Research and present on a person who took bold action to achieve success.

Start where you are. Use what you have. Do what you can.– Arthur Ashe

Day 190

Building Confidence Through Affirmation and Posture

Morning Pause: Affirm: "I am capable of achieving great things."

Noon Pause: Take a walk while repeating your affirmation and noticing how your posture shifts.

Evening Pause: Reflect: How did moving with confidence impact your mindset?

Classroom Activity: Power Posing—students practice using posture to enhance confidence.

Believe in yourself and all that you are. Know that there is something inside you that is greater than any obstacle.- Christian D. Larson

Day 191

Overcoming Fear and Building Confidence

Morning Pause: Close your eyes and visualize success in a current challenge.

Noon Pause: Write down a fear you overcame this week and celebrate the progress.

Evening Pause: Reflect: How does taking action reduce fear over time?

Classroom Activity: Reflection Discussion—Students share their biggest confidence-building moments so far.

Fear is only as deep as the mind allows. – Japanese Proverb

Day 192

Taking Inspired Action Despite Fear

Morning Pause: Set an intention to take one bold step today.

Noon Pause: List three fears and write one step you can take to face each.

Evening Pause: Reflect: What action did you take, and how did it feel?

Classroom Activity: Fear to Fuel—Students identify a past fear they overcame and share their story.

Everything you want is on the other side of fear.– Jack Canfield

Day 193

Cultivating Courage and Clarity

Morning Pause: Repeat: "I act with courage and clarity."

Noon Pause: Take five deep breaths and visualize yourself achieving a goal.

Evening Pause: Reflect: How did visualization strengthen your resolve?

Classroom Activity: Success Mindset—Students set a short-term goal and map action steps.

Courage is resistance to fear, mastery of fear, not absence of fear.– Mark Twain

Day 194

Embracing Discomfort for Growth

Morning Pause: Affirm: "I am fearless in pursuit of my dreams."

Noon Pause: Step outside your comfort zone in a tiny way.

Evening Pause: Reflect: What did you learn by stepping into discomfort?

Classroom Activity: Comfort Zone Challenge—students attempt an unfamiliar task.

If you want something you've never had, you must be willing to do something you've never done. – Thomas Jefferson

Day 195

Resilience Through Setbacks

Morning Pause: Meditate on resilience—imagine yourself overcoming obstacles.

Noon Pause: Write down a moment when you turned failure into growth.

Evening Pause: Reflect: How do setbacks shape strength?

Classroom Activity: Growth Mindset—Students discuss lessons from failure.

Our greatest glory is not in never falling, but in rising every time we fall. – Confucius.

Day 196

Cultivating Courage in Leadership

Morning Pause: Set an intention to lead with courage today.

Noon Pause: Encourage someone or take a leadership role in a small way.

Evening Pause: Reflect: How did demonstrating courage impact your day?

Classroom Activity: Leadership role-play scenarios to practice decision-making under pressure.

Courage is resistance to fear, mastery of fear—not absence of fear. – Mark Twain

Day 197

Embracing Your Authentic Power & Leadership

Morning Pause (5 min): Set an intention to show up as your most authentic self today.

Noon Pause (5-10 min): Identify a moment where you held back your voice and reflect on how you can speak up next time.

Evening Pause (3-5 min): Reflect: How did you honor your authentic self today?

Classroom Activity: Group discussion on what authenticity means and why it matters.

Be yourself; everyone else is already taken. – Oscar Wilde

Day 198

Cultivating Self-Trust

Morning Pause: Affirm: "I trust myself to make the right choices."

Noon Pause: Think of a past decision that led to positive growth and appreciate your wisdom.

Evening Pause: Reflect: How does trusting yourself impact your confidence?

Classroom Activity: Students write a letter to their future selves offering encouragement and wisdom.

Self-trust is the first secret of success. – Ralph Waldo Emerson

Day 199

Leading by Example

Morning Pause: Meditate on the phrase: "I am a leader in my own life."

Noon Pause: Identify one small way you can lead by example today.

Evening Pause: Reflect: What does leadership mean to you, and how do you embody it?

Classroom Activity: Leadership Circle—Students share qualities of great leaders.

The most powerful leadership tool you have is your example.– John Wooden

Day 200

The Power of Resilience

Morning Pause: Breathe deeply and embrace the mindset of resilience.

Noon Pause: Recall a past challenge that made you stronger—write down the lesson you gained.

Evening Pause: Reflect: How does resilience shape the way you handle fear and confidence?

Classroom Activity: Resilience storytelling—students share a time they overcame adversity.

Do not judge me by my success; judge me by how many times I fell and got back up again. – Nelson Mandela

Day 201

Embracing Self-Worth

Morning Pause: Affirm: "I release the need for outside validation. My worth comes from within."

Noon Pause: Notice any moments today when you sought approval from others—how did it affect you?

Evening Pause: Reflect: What happens when you validate yourself instead of seeking it from others?

Classroom Activity: Self-Appreciation Exercise—Students list five things they admire about themselves.

No one can make you feel inferior without your consent. – Eleanor Roosevelt

Day 202

Embracing Change with Confidence

Morning Pause: Meditate on the phrase: "I embrace change as an opportunity for growth."

Noon Pause: Identify one change happening in your life and find one positive aspect of it.

Evening Pause: Reflect: How does shifting your perspective on change impact your confidence?

Classroom Activity: Change Challenge—Students discuss how to adapt to new situations with confidence.

Change is the law of life. And those who look only to the past or present are certain to miss the future. – John F. Kennedy.

Day 203

Stepping Into Your Confidence

Morning Pause: Close your eyes and visualize yourself confidently navigating a future challenge.

Noon Pause: Write a note of encouragement to yourself for when you face self-doubt.

Evening Pause: Reflect: What have you learned about yourself in these 28 days of practicing confidence?

Classroom Activity: Reflection journal—Students write about their biggest takeaways from the journey.

You are braver than you believe, stronger than you seem, and smarter than you think.- A.A. Milne

Day 204

Finding Joy in Small Moments

Morning Pause: Breathe deeply, smile, and set an intention to find joy in small moments.

Noon Pause: Step outside or look around, take five deep breaths, and notice something beautiful. Stretch and release tension.

Evening Pause: Reflect on three joyful moments from today. Express gratitude.

Classroom Activity: Have students share one small thing that made them smile today.

Happiness is created through your actions. —
Dalai Lama

Day 205

Embracing Playfulness

Morning Pause (5 min): Begin the day with a gentle smile and three deep breaths. Affirm: "I create joy through my thoughts and actions."

Noon Pause (5-10 min): Take a mindful walk, paying attention to colors and sounds. If indoors, do a quick movement exercise like stretching or yoga.

Evening Pause (3-5 min): Close your eyes and visualize a happy memory. Feel the joy from that moment fill your heart.

The more you appreciate and embrace life's moments, the more joy and abundance you create.
— Kim Groshek

Day 206

Practicing Gratitude

Morning Pause (5 min): Begin with three deep breaths and a light stretch. Say: "I welcome joy into my day."

Noon Pause (5-10 min): Write down three things you are grateful for. Read them slowly, feeling appreciation for each one.

Evening Pause (3-5 min): Listen to a calming piece of music. Let the rhythm guide your breath and relaxation.

Find out where joy resides and give it a voice far beyond singing. For to miss the joy is to miss all.—Robert Louis Stevenson.

Day 207

Laughing More

Morning Pause: Start with a smile and three deep breaths. Say: "I allow playfulness to brighten my day."

Noon Pause: Watch a short, funny video or recall a humorous memory. Laugh freely.

Evening Pause: Reflect on what made you smile today and hold onto that feeling.

Classroom Activity: Have a "laughter circle" where students share funny stories or jokes to boost joy and connection.

A day without laughter is a day wasted.— Charlie Chaplin

Day 208

Finding Success in Joy

Morning Pause (5 min): Deep breath in, deep breath out. Affirm: "My happiness fuels my success."

Noon Pause (5-10 min): Recall a past success and the joy it brought. Write down what contributed to that success.

Evening Pause (3-5 min): Close your eyes and visualize your future success. Feel the happiness that comes with achieving it.

Success is not the key to happiness. Happiness is the key to success. — Albert Schweitzer.

Day 209

Spreading Positivity

Morning Pause: Breathe deeply and set an intention: "Today, I will spread joy."

Noon Pause: Perform a small act of kindness (a compliment, a thank-you, or a helping hand). Notice how it makes you feel.

Evening Pause: Reflect on how you brought joy to others today. Express gratitude for the opportunity to share positivity.

Classroom Activity: Have students write anonymous kindness notes to classmates and share how it felt to give and receive positivity.

"Lifting others lifts us all." — Kim Groshek.

Day 210

Reflecting on Joy

Morning Pause: Breathe deeply and affirm, "I welcome joy into my life."

Noon Pause: Record a joyful moment from each day this week. Reflect on what brings you happiness.

Evening Pause: Smile, close your eyes, and plan a joyful activity for next week.

Classroom Activity: Create a "Joy Jar" where students collect and share happy moments.

Joy grows when we take time to notice it.— Kim Groshek.

Day 211

Embracing Daily Joy

Morning Pause: Start with a gentle smile and three deep breaths. Affirm, "I create joy through my thoughts and actions."

Noon Pause: Take a mindful walk, noticing colors and sounds. If indoors, do light stretching or yoga.

Evening Pause: Close your eyes, recall a happy memory, and let joy fill your heart.

Classroom Activity: 3-Minute Journaling—Students write down one thing that made them smile today.

The more you celebrate life, the more there is to celebrate. —Kim Groshek.

Day 212

Inviting Joy into Your Day

Morning Pause: Begin with three deep breaths and a light stretch. Say: "I welcome joy into my day."

Noon Pause: Write down three things you are grateful for. Read them slowly, feeling appreciation for each one.

Evening Pause: Listen to a calming piece of music. Let the rhythm guide your breath and relaxation.

Classroom Practice: Group Gratitude Circle: Students share one joyful moment in pairs.

Joy thrives where gratitude grows—embrace it, celebrate it, and let it shine.— Kim Groshek

Day 213

Practicing Laughter & Play

Morning Pause (5 min): Start with a smile and three deep breaths. Say: "I allow playfulness to brighten my day."

Noon Pause (5-10 min): Watch a short, funny video or recall a humorous memory. Allow yourself to laugh freely.

Evening Pause (3-5 min): Reflect: What made me smile today? Hold onto that feeling as you unwind.

Classroom Practice: Laughter Challenge: Students share a joke or a funny story with the class.

A day without laughter is a day wasted.— Charlie Chaplin

Day 214

The Link Between Happiness & Success

Morning Pause (5 min): Breathe deeply and affirm, "My happiness fuels my success."

Noon Pause (5-10 min): Reflect on a past success and the joy it brought. Write down what contributed to it.

Evening Pause (3-5 min): Visualize your future success and embrace the happiness it brings.

Classroom Activity: Students create a vision board representing success and happiness.

Happiness is the foundation where success thrives.
— Kim Groshek.

Day 215

Spreading Joy in the Classroom/Workplace

Morning Pause (5 min): Breathe in deeply and set an intention: "Today, I will spread joy."

Noon Pause (5-10 min): Perform one small act of kindness (a compliment, a thank-you, a helping hand). Notice how it makes you feel.

Evening Pause (3-5 min): Reflect: How did I bring joy to others today? Express gratitude for the opportunity to share positivity.

Classroom Practice: Secret Kindness Mission: Each student draws a name and does one kind act for that person during the day.

We rise by lifting others. — Robert Ingersoll

Day 216

Overcoming Money Blocks Through Mindfulness

Morning Pause (5 min): Breathe deeply, reflect on money beliefs, and replace negativity with positive affirmations.

Noon Pause (5-10 min): Visualize money as abundant energy and reframe limiting beliefs.

Evening Pause (3-5 min): List three financial gratitudes, release guilt, and affirm, "I am worthy of abundance."

Classroom: Discuss money beliefs and create affirmations.

Abundance begins with a mindset shift. — Kim Groshek.

Day 217

Overcoming Money Blocks Through Mindfulness

Morning: Reflect on early money memories, identify limiting beliefs, and reframe them with positive affirmations.

Afternoon: Visualize money as abundant energy. Observe thoughts about wealth and journal mindset shifts.

Evening: List three financial gratitudes, release guilt, and affirm abundance.

Classroom Activity: Discuss money beliefs and create personal affirmations.

We attract abundance when we believe we deserve it. — Kim Groshek.

Day 218

Overcoming Money Blocks Through Mindfulness

Morning: Reflect on early money memories. Identify and reframe limiting beliefs with positive affirmations.

Afternoon: Visualize money as energy, observe thoughts, and journal mindset shifts.

Evening: List three financial gratitudes. Release guilt or resentment. Affirm: "I am worthy of financial abundance."

Classroom Activity: Discuss money beliefs and write affirmations.

Abundance starts with a mindset. — Kim Groshek.

Day 219

Overcoming Money Blocks Through Mindfulness

Morning: Visualize abundance, reframe one limiting belief, and set a mindful financial intention.

Afternoon: Make a conscious financial choice, observe emotions, and celebrate small wins.

Evening: Reflect on a financial blessing, read a success story, and affirm: *"I welcome wealth with gratitude."*

Activity: Write a letter to your future successful self about financial goals.

Abundance grows with an aligned mindset and action.—Kim Groshek.

Day 220

Overcoming Money Blocks Through Mindfulness

Morning: Release money stress with deep breaths, create a financial mantra, and acknowledge abundance.

Afternoon: Practice generosity, visualize financial security, and notice abundance around you.

Evening: Reflect on a positive financial memory, release one fear, and affirm: *"Abundance is all around me."*

Activity: Create a vision board for financial success.

Abundance flows through gratitude and possibility.
— Kim Groshek

Day 221

Overcoming Money Blocks Through Mindfulness

Morning: List three financial gratitudes, meditate on abundance, and set a wealth-building intention.

Afternoon: Shift mindset—replace *"I can't afford this"* with *"How can I?"* Reflect on money patterns and read an inspiring story.

Evening: Celebrate a financial lesson, meditate on peace, and affirm: *"Money is unlimited, and I attract it easily."*

Activity: Discuss successful money habits.

Wealth begins with abundance. — Kim Groshek

Day 222

Overcoming Money Blocks Through Mindfulness

Morning (15 min): Set a financial intention. Reflect on goals. Repeat a positive money mantra.

Afternoon (15 min): Make a mindful spending choice. Recognize abundance. Track progress.

Evening (15 min): Write about financial gratitude. Read a success story. Affirm: "I am financially free."

Classroom Activity: Students write an abundance journal entry.

Abundance flows when we align our mindset with possibility.— Kim Groshek

Day 223

Daily Gratitude for Financial Abundance

Morning (15 min): Write three things you appreciate about your finances. Breathe deeply and focus on abundance. Set an intention for financial gratitude.

Afternoon (15 min): Practice generosity, take a gratitude walk, and celebrate financial wins.

Evening (15 min): Write a thank-you note to money and meditate on wealth. Affirm: "I am grateful for the financial prosperity in my life."

Gratitude for your financial journey attracts more abundance. — Kim Groshek.

Day 224

Daily Gratitude for Financial Abundance

Morning (15 min): List five financial blessings, big or small. Visualize your dream abundant life. Set a financial action intention for the day.

Afternoon (15 min): Take an abundance walk, practice generosity, and track financial wins.

Evening (15 min): Reflect on your financial gratitude, read a success story, and affirm: "I am grateful for the wealth flowing into my life."

Gratitude fuels financial prosperity and unlocks new opportunities.— Kim Groshek

Day 225

Entrepreneurial Mindset Shifts for Success

Morning: Reframe a limiting belief, review your vision board, and ask, "What action brings me closer to success?"

Afternoon: List three successful qualities, learn about wealth, and connect with a mentor.

Evening: Celebrate a financial action, meditate on growth, and affirm, "I am creating unlimited wealth."

Classroom: Assign a business idea project.

Success is not in what you have but who you are.–
Bo Bennett

Day 226

The Habits of Wealthy, Mindful Leaders

Morning: Adopt a wealthy habit, review finances calmly, and set a wealth-building intention.

Afternoon: Spend intentionally, give meaningfully, and grow with a financial podcast.

Evening: Track progress, appreciate growth, and affirm: *"I am a wealthy, mindful leader creating abundance."*

Activity: Discuss leaders' habits and set financial goals.

"Abundance flows when we align with our mindset and action." — Kim Groshek.

Day 227

Reflection, Celebration, and Looking Ahead

Morning: Breathe deeply, reflect on key accomplishments.

Noon: Write down three achievements from the past year.

Evening: Express gratitude for lessons learned.

Classroom Practice: List five personal strengths and discuss.

Growth is never by mere chance; it is the result of forces working together.– James Cash Penney

Day 228

Reviewing Personal Growth Over the Year

Morning: Meditate on a defining moment of growth.

Noon: Share a success story with someone.

Evening: Journal about a challenge that made you stronger.

Classroom Practice: Identify a role model and their key traits.

Success is not final, failure is not fatal: it is the courage to continue that counts." – Winston Churchill

Day 229

Reviewing Personal Growth Over the Year

Morning: Set an intention to acknowledge your progress.

Noon: Write a thank-you note to yourself.

Evening: Reflect on how you've changed over the year.

Classroom Practice: Write a short essay on personal growth.

Strive not to be a success but rather to be of value.– Albert Einstein

Day 230

Practicing Deep Gratitude for 365 Days of Pause

Morning. Reflect on three things for which you are grateful.

Noon: Practice a five-minute gratitude meditation.

Evening: Share a moment of gratitude with a friend.

Classroom Practice: Write gratitude letters to classmates.

Gratitude turns what we have into enough." –
Melody Beattie

Day 231

Practicing Deep Gratitude for 365 Days of Pause

Morning. Acknowledge a person who impacted your year.

Noon: Create a gratitude list of at least ten items.

Evening: Say thank you to someone meaningful.

Classroom Practice: Gratitude circle—each student shares one thing they appreciate.

"Gratitude is the pause that helps us appreciate the abundance around us." — Kim Groshek.

Day 232

Setting Mindful Goals for the New Year

Morning: Visualize your ideal future.

Noon: Write down three goals for the next year.

Evening: Identify one small step toward a goal.

Classroom Practice: Vision board activity.

A goal properly set is halfway reached. – Zig Ziglar

Day 233

Setting Mindful Goals for the New Year

Morning: Set a clear intention for personal growth.

Noon: Reflect on an area for improvement.

Evening: Write a commitment to self-growth.

Classroom Practice: SMART goal-setting session.

The only limit to our realization of tomorrow is our doubts of today.– Franklin D. Roosevelt

Day 234

Creating a Lifelong Practice of Pausing

Morning: Commit to a daily pause habit.

Noon: Reflect on how pausing has benefited you.

Evening: Write a self-affirmation.

Classroom Practice: Group discussion on the power of pausing.

Almost everything will work again if you unplug it for a few minutes, including you. – Anne Lamott

Day 235

Reviewing Personal Growth Over the Year

Morning Pause (5 min): Engage in mindful breathing, focusing on the present moment.

Noon Pause (5-10 min): List three skills you've developed this year.

Evening Pause (3-5 min): Reflect on a recent success and the effort it took.

Classroom Practice: Students pair up to discuss personal achievements.

Success is not the key to happiness. Happiness is the key to success. – Albert Schweitzer

Day 236

Reviewing Personal Growth Over the Year

Morning Pause (5 min): Visualize overcoming a past obstacle.

Noon Pause (5-10 min): Write about a lesson learned from failure.

Evening Pause (3-5 min): Express gratitude for supportive people in your life.

Classroom Practice: Group discussion on turning failures into learning opportunities.

Failure is simply the opportunity to begin again, this time more intelligently. – Henry Ford

Day 237

Reviewing Personal Growth Over the Year

Morning Pause (5 min): Set an intention to embrace challenges today.

Noon Pause (5-10 min): Identify a recent challenge and brainstorm solutions.

Evening Pause (3-5 min): Reflect on how you've grown from a specific experience.

Classroom Practice: Students create a "growth timeline" highlighting key personal events.

Challenges are what make life interesting; overcoming them is what makes life meaningful. – Joshua J. Marine

Day 238

Reviewing Personal Growth Over the Year

Morning Pause (5 min): Meditate on your values.

Noon Pause (5-10 min): Write about how your actions align with your values.

Evening Pause (3-5 min): Acknowledge a value you upheld today.

Classroom Practice: Students list their core values and share examples of living them.

Your values create your internal compass that can navigate how you make decisions in your life. – Roy T. Bennett

Day 239

Reviewing Personal Growth Over the Year

Morning Pause (5 min): Reflect on a time you stepped out of your comfort zone.

Noon Pause (5-10 min): Plan a small action that challenges you.

Evening Pause (3-5 min): Journal about the feelings associated with taking risks.

Classroom Practice: Role-playing scenarios that encourage stepping beyond comfort zones.

Life begins at the end of your comfort zone. – Neale Donald Walsch

Day 240

Reviewing Personal Growth Over the Year

Morning Pause (5 min): Visualize your proudest moment this year.

Noon Pause (5-10 min): Share this moment with a friend or colleague.

Evening Pause (3-5 min): Express gratitude for the journey to that achievement.

Classroom Practice: Students present their proudest moments to the class.

Take pride in how far you have come, and have faith in how far you can go. – Christian Larson

Day 241

Reviewing Personal Growth Over the Year

Morning Pause (5 min): Set an intention to recognize growth in others.

Noon Pause (5-10 min): Compliment someone on their progress.

Evening Pause (3-5 min): Reflect on how supporting others enhances your growth.

Classroom Practice: Peer review sessions highlighting each other's improvements.

We rise by lifting others. – Robert Ingersoll

Day 242

Practicing Deep Gratitude for 365 Days of Pause

Morning Pause (5 min): Reflect on the simple joys in your life.

Noon Pause (5-10 min): Write a thank-you note to someone who made you smile.

Evening Pause (3-5 min): Express gratitude for a recent positive experience.

Classroom Practice: Create a "Gratitude Wall" where students post notes of thanks.

Enjoy the little things, and for one day, you may look back and realize they were the big things.–
Robert Brault

Day 243

Practicing Deep Gratitude for 365 Days of Pause

Morning Pause (5 min): Acknowledge the support system around you.

Noon Pause (5-10 min): Reach out to a mentor or friend to express appreciation.

Evening Pause (3-5 min): Reflect on how others' support has impacted your journey.

Classroom Practice: Students write letters to someone who has influenced them positively.

A mentor is someone who allows you to see the hope inside yourself. – Oprah Winfrey

Day 244

Practicing Deep Gratitude for 365 Days of Pause

Morning Pause (5 min): Consider the opportunities you've received this year.

Noon Pause (5-10 min): Write about an opportunity that led to personal growth.

Evening Pause (3-5 min): Express gratitude for the chance to learn from new experiences.

Classroom Practice: Group discussion on seizing opportunities and their outcomes.

Opportunities don't just happen. You create them.– Chris Grosser

Day 245

Practicing Deep Gratitude for 365 Days of Pause

Morning Pause (5 min): Reflect on the beauty of nature around you.

Noon Pause (5-10 min): Take a mindful walk, appreciating your surroundings.

Evening Pause (3-5 min): Journal about how nature inspires gratitude in you.

Classroom Practice: Students share experiences of connecting with nature.

Look deep into nature, and then you will understand everything better. – Albert Einstein

Day 246

Practicing Deep Gratitude for 365 Days of Pause

Morning Pause (5 min): Think about a recent act of kindness you received.

Noon Pause (5-10 min): Perform a random act of kindness for someone else.

Evening Pause (3-5 min): Reflect on how kindness impacts both the giver and the receiver.

Classroom Practice: Plan a class project focused on community service.

No act of kindness, no matter how small, is ever wasted. – Aesop

Day 247

Practicing Deep Gratitude for 365 Days of Pause

Morning Pause (5 min): Acknowledge a personal strength you're grateful for.

Noon Pause (5-10 min): Share this strength with someone and how it has helped you.

Evening Pause (3-5 min): Reflect on how utilizing your strengths has shaped your year.

Classroom Practice: Students identify and discuss their unique strengths in small groups.

What lies behind us and what lies before us are tiny matters compared to what lies within us. – Ralph Waldo Emerson

Day 248

Setting Mindful Goals for the New Year

Morning Pause (5 min): Visualize your ideal self in the coming year.

Noon Pause (5-10 min): Set three specific, achievable goals aligned with this vision.

Evening Pause (3-5 min): Write down one action you can take tomorrow toward these goals.

Classroom Practice: Workshop on setting SMART (Specific, Measurable, Achievable, Relevant, Time-bound) goals.

Setting goals is the first step in turning the invisible into the visible. – Tony Robbins

Day 249

Setting Mindful Goals for the New Year

Morning Pause (5 min): Reflect on past goals you've achieved and how they benefited you.

Noon Pause (5-10 min): Identify potential obstacles to your new goals and brainstorm solutions.

Evening Pause (3-5 min): Commit to a positive mindset in overcoming challenges.

Classroom Practice: Students create action plans detailing steps to achieve their goals.

Obstacles are those frightful things you see when you take your eyes off your goal. – Henry Ford

Day 250

Setting Mindful Goals for the New Year

Morning Pause (5 min): Consider habits that support your goals.

Noon Pause (5-10 min): Plan how to incorporate a new positive habit into your routine.

Evening Pause (3-5 min): Reflect on the importance of consistency in habit formation.

Classroom Practice: Discussion on habit-building and its impact on goal achievement.

Excellence is not a single act but a way of being—shaped by the habits we choose every day. – Kim Groshek

Day 251

Creating a Lifelong Practice of Pausing

Morning Pause (5 min): Reflect on the joy of giving and receiving.

Noon Pause (5-10 min): Share a moment of kindness with someone today.

Evening Pause (3-5 min): Express gratitude for the connections made throughout the year.

Classroom Practice: Students discuss the importance of generosity and plan a small act of kindness as a group.

It's not how much we give but how much love we put into giving. – Mother Teresa

Day 252

Creating a Lifelong Practice of Pausing

Morning Pause (5 min): Consider the lessons learned from challenges faced this year.

Noon Pause (5-10 min): Write about a challenge that led to personal growth.

Evening Pause (3-5 min): Acknowledge your resilience and strength.

Classroom Practice: Students share stories of overcoming obstacles and the lessons gained.

The greater the obstacle, the more glory in overcoming it. – Molière

Day 253

Creating a Lifelong Practice of Pausing

Morning Pause (5 min): Visualize the habits you wish to cultivate in the coming year.

Noon Pause (5-10 min): Identify one habit to focus on and outline steps to integrate it into your routine.

Evening Pause (3-5 min): Reflect on the benefits this new habit will bring to your life.

Classroom Practice: Students set personal development goals and create action plans.

We are what we repeatedly do. Excellence, then, is not an act but a habit.– Aristotle

Day 254

Creating a Lifelong Practice of Pausing

Morning Pause (5 min): Think about the people who have supported you this year.

Noon Pause (5-10 min): Reach out to someone and express your appreciation for their support.

Evening Pause (3-5 min): Reflect on how these relationships have enriched your life.

Classroom Practice: Students write thank-you notes to individuals who have positively influenced them.

Appreciation can make a day and even change a life. Your willingness to put it into words is all that is necessary. – Margaret Cousins

Day 255

Creating a Lifelong Practice of Pausing

Morning Pause (5 min): Contemplate the importance of self-care and well-being.

Noon Pause (5-10 min): Engage in an activity that rejuvenates your mind and body.

Evening Pause (3-5 min): Plan regular self-care routines for the upcoming year.

Classroom Practice: Discussion on the significance of self-care and students create personal wellness plans.

Self-care is not selfish. You cannot serve from an empty vessel.– Eleanor Brownn

Day 256

Creating a Lifelong Practice of Pausing

Morning Pause: Reflect on your growth over the past month.

Noon Pause: Celebrate your achievements and set intentions to continue pausing.

Evening Pause: Express gratitude for your commitment to well-being.

Classroom Activity: Group reflection—students share insights from their journey.

Every great journey begins with a single step. –
Lao Tzu

Day 257

Building Habits That Stick

Morning Pause (5 min): Identify a simple habit you wish to develop this month.

Noon Pause (5-10 min): Visualize the positive impact this habit will have on your life.

Evening Pause (3-5 min): Record your commitment to this habit in a journal.

Classroom Practice: Introduce the 30-Day Habit Challenge; students select a personal habit to track daily.

We are what we repeatedly do. Excellence, then, is not an act, but a habit. – Aristotle.

Day 258

Building Habits That Stick

Morning Pause (5 min): Set a specific time each day dedicated to your new habit.

Noon Pause (5-10 min): Reflect on potential obstacles and plan strategies to overcome them.

Evening Pause (3-5 min): Acknowledge your effort in practicing the habit today.

Classroom Practice: Students share their chosen habits and discuss possible challenges and solutions.

Motivation is what gets you started. Habit is what keeps you going. – Jim Ryun

Day 259

Building Habits That Stick

Morning Pause (5 min): Reaffirm your commitment to your habit with a positive affirmation.

Noon Pause (5-10 min): Engage in a brief mindfulness exercise to center your focus.

Evening Pause (3-5 min): Note any progress or difficulties encountered.

Classroom Practice: Teach students about the habit loop: cue, routine, reward.

The chains of habit are too weak to be felt until they are too strong to be broken. – Samuel Johnson

Day 260

Building Habits That Stick

Morning Pause (5 min): Visualize successfully integrating your habit into your daily routine.

Noon Pause (5-10 min): Identify a reward for consistently practicing your habit.

Evening Pause (3-5 min): Reflect on the day's successes and areas for improvement.

Classroom Practice: Students create a visual tracker to monitor their habit progress.

Your net worth to the world is usually determined by what remains after your bad habits are subtracted from your good ones. – Benjamin Franklin

Day 261

Building Habits That Stick

Morning Pause (5 min): Recall the reasons why this habit is important to you.

Noon Pause (5-10 min): Share your habit journey with a friend or mentor for accountability.

Evening Pause (3-5 min): Express gratitude for the opportunity to grow through this habit.

Classroom Practice: Pair students as accountability partners to support each other's habit development.

Discipline is the bridge between goals and accomplishment.– Jim Rohn

Day 262

Building Habits That Stick

Morning Pause (5 min): Set a mini-goal related to your habit for the upcoming week.

Noon Pause (5-10 min): Reflect on the feelings and benefits experienced from practicing your habit.

Evening Pause (3-5 min): Document any triggers that make practicing your habit easier or harder.

Classroom Practice: Discuss the role of triggers in habit formation and how to create positive cues.

Success is the sum of small efforts, repeated day in and day out. – Robert Collier

Day 263

Building Habits That Stick

Morning Pause (5 min): Review your progress from the past week and celebrate small victories.

Noon Pause (5-10 min): Adjust your strategies if needed to enhance habit adherence.

Evening Pause (3-5 min): Set intentions for the upcoming week to continue building your habit.

Classroom Practice: Students reflect on their first week, sharing successes and areas for improvement.

First, we form habits, and then they form us. Conquer your bad habits, or they will conquer you.– Rob Gilbert

Day 264

The Science of Motivation

Morning Pause (5 min): Reflect on what drives you to pursue your goals.

Noon Pause (5-10 min): Identify intrinsic and extrinsic motivators in your life.

Evening Pause (3-5 min): Journal about a time when motivation led you to success.

Classroom Practice: Introduce the concept of intrinsic vs. extrinsic motivation; students list examples of each.

People often say that motivation doesn't last. Well, neither does bathing—that's why we recommend it daily. – Zig Ziglar

Day 265

The Science of Motivation

Morning Pause (5 min): Set an intention to notice moments of natural motivation today.

Noon Pause (5-10 min): Reflect on activities that energize and inspire you.

Evening Pause (3-5 min): Journal about a motivational experience from the day.

Classroom Practice: Students discuss personal motivators and how they influence behavior.

The only way to do great work is to love what you do. – Steve Jobs

Day 266

The Science of Motivation

Morning Pause (5 min): Recall a past achievement and the motivation behind it.

Noon Pause (5-10 min): Identify a current goal and the intrinsic motivations driving it.

Evening Pause (3-5 min): Write down one thing that inspired you today.

Classroom Practice: Introduce vision boards; students begin collecting images and quotes that represent their goals.

Success is not the key to happiness. Happiness is the key to success.– Albert Schweitzer

Day 267

The Science of Motivation

Morning Pause (5 min): Visualize achieving a current goal and the feelings associated with it.

Noon Pause (5-10 min): Consider how your environment affects your motivation.

Evening Pause (3-5 min): Note any changes you can make to boost motivation.

Classroom Practice: Students create their vision boards, focusing on personal and academic aspirations.

Your only limitation is the one you create in your mind.– Kim Groshek

Day 268

The Science of Motivation

Morning Pause (5 min): Affirm your ability to overcome challenges.

Noon Pause (5-10 min): Reflect on a time when perseverance led to success.

Evening Pause (3-5 min): Write about a challenge you're currently facing and potential solutions.

Classroom Practice: Students present their vision boards and discuss the motivations behind their chosen goals.

Dream it. Believe in it. Take action to make it real.
– Kim Groshek

Day 269

The Science of Motivation

Morning Pause (5 min): Set a small, achievable goal for the day.

Noon Pause (5-10 min): Break down a larger goal into manageable steps.

Evening Pause (3-5 min): Acknowledge the completion of today's goal and plan for tomorrow.

Classroom Practice: Teach students about SMART goals; they apply this framework to one of their aspirations.

Stay focused, go after your dreams, and keep moving toward your goals. – LL Cool J

Day 270

The Science of Motivation

Morning Pause (5 min): Reflect on the progress made this week.

Noon Pause (5-10 min): Identify any obstacles encountered and how you addressed them.

Evening Pause (3-5 min): Express gratitude for the lessons learned through challenges.

Classroom Practice: Students share their SMART goals and discuss potential challenges and solutions.

The effort you put in today will make your achievements feel even more rewarding tomorrow.
– Kim Groshek.

Day 271

Building Resilience Through Challenges

Morning Pause: Reflect on a recent setback and how you overcame it.

Noon Pause: Identify support systems that help you during tough times.

Evening Pause: Journal about the strengths that aid your resilience.

Classroom Practice: Introduce resilience; students share personal stories of overcoming challenges.

Strength does not come from winning. Your struggles develop your strengths." – Arnold Schwarzenegger.

Day 272

Embracing Challenges for Growth and Resilience

Morning Pause: Set an intention to embrace challenges as growth opportunities.

Noon Pause: Reflect on a challenging situation and its lessons.

Evening Pause: Write about how you can apply these lessons to current challenges.

Classroom Practice: Students discuss resilience strategies and coping mechanisms.

The comeback is always stronger than the setback.
– Kim Groshek

Day 273

Resilience in Difficult Times

Morning Pause: Visualize yourself overcoming a current challenge.

Noon Pause: Identify emotions tied to this challenge and how to manage them.

Evening Pause: Journal your most effective coping strategies.

Classroom Practice: Teach stress management techniques; students practice deep breathing.

Hard times may have held you down, but they will not last forever. – Kim Groshek

Day 274

Building Resilience Through Challenges

Morning Pause: Reflect on a recent challenge and how you overcame it.

Noon Pause: Identify a current obstacle and brainstorm possible solutions.

Evening Pause: Journal about the strengths you used today.

Classroom Practice: Students share stories of resilience and discuss coping strategies.

Strength does not come from winning. Your struggles develop your strengths. – Arnold Schwarzenegger

Day 275

Embracing Challenges and Learning from Failure

Morning Pause: Set an intention to view challenges as opportunities.

Noon Pause: Reflect on a past failure and the lessons learned.

Evening Pause: Write about how you applied a lesson from failure today.

Classroom Practice: A group discussion on famous figures who turned failures into successes.

A comeback is always stronger than a setback.–
Kim Groshek

Day 276

Resilience in Difficult Times

Morning Pause: Visualize overcoming challenges for 5 minutes.

Noon Pause: Acknowledge your emotions and create coping strategies.

Evening Pause: Journal about coping techniques and practice deep breathing.

Classroom Practice: Teach stress management and lead deep breathing exercises.

Though adversity might temporarily ground you, it will never last—your inner strength will always lift you toward a brighter tomorrow.– Kim Groshek

Day 277

Resilience in Difficult Times

Morning Pause (5 min): Affirm your resilience and ability to adapt.

Noon Pause (5-10 min): Recall a time when adaptability led to success.

Evening Pause (3-5 min): Write about how you adapted to a situation today.

Classroom Practice: Students role-play scenarios requiring adaptability.

Adaptability is about the powerful difference between adapting to cope and adapting to win. – Max McKeown

Day 278

Resilience in Difficult Times

Morning Pause (5 min): Set an intention to seek support when needed.

Noon Pause (5-10 min): Identify your support network and how they assist you.

Evening Pause (3-5 min): Express gratitude for someone who supported you today.

Classroom Practice: Students write thank-you notes to someone who has helped them.

Alone, we can do so little; together, we can do so much. – Helen Keller

Day 279

Resilience in Difficult Times

Morning Pause (5 min): Reflect on a recent success and the effort it took.

Noon Pause (5-10 min): Break down a current goal into actionable steps.

Evening Pause (3-5 min): Acknowledge the progress made toward this goal today.

Classroom Practice: Students set short-term goals and outline steps to achieve them.

Success is the sum of small efforts, repeated day in and day out. – Robert Collier

Day 280

Resilience in Difficult Times

Morning Pause (5 min): Visualize the completion of a major goal.

Noon Pause (5-10 min): Identify potential distractions and plan to minimize them.

Evening Pause (3-5 min): Reflect on how you stayed focused today.

Classroom Practice: Discuss time management techniques and their application.

The secret of your future is hidden in your daily routine.– Mike Murdock

Day 281

Staying Committed to Your Goals

Morning Pause (5 min): Reaffirm your commitment to a specific goal.

Noon Pause (5-10 min): Identify any habits that hinder your progress.

Evening Pause (3-5 min): Plan how to replace one unproductive habit with a productive one.

Classroom Practice: Students discuss common bad habits and brainstorm replacement behaviors.

We are what we repeatedly do. Excellence, then, is not an act, but a habit.– Aristotle

Day 282

Staying Committed to Your Goals

Morning Pause (5 min): Visualize overcoming a temptation that distracts you from your goals.

Noon Pause (5-10 min): Reflect on situations where you've successfully resisted temptations.

Evening Pause (3-5 min): Journal about a temptation you faced today and how you handled it.

Classroom Practice: Role-play scenarios where students practice saying no to distractions.

Discipline is choosing between what you want now and what you want most." – Abraham Lincoln.

Day 283

Cultivating Mindfulness

Morning Pause: Breathe deeply and set an intention for mindfulness.

Noon Pause: Practice mindfulness, observing thoughts and sensations without judgment.

Evening Pause: Reflect on mindful moments and list three things you're grateful for.

Classroom Activity: Lead a breathing exercise to enhance focus.

Mindfulness is the key to unlocking the door to abundance – Kim Groshek.

Day 284

Observing Thoughts

Morning Pause: Focus on your breath, letting thoughts pass without attachment. Set an intention to observe your thoughts.

Noon Pause (5 min): Observe your thoughts non-judgmentally, letting recurring ones fade.

Evening Pause (3 min): Reflect on your thought patterns. Acknowledge positive ones and express gratitude.

Classroom Activity: Have students write down their thoughts and reflect.

Your thoughts create your reality. – Kim Groshek

Day 285

Body Awareness

Morning Pause: Do a body scan from head to toe, setting an intention to stay present in your body.

Noon Pause: Notice areas of tension, breathe into them, and release with each exhale.

Evening Pause: Reflect on your body's sensations and express gratitude for its strength.

Classroom Activity: Guide students through a body scan to enhance awareness.

Take care of your body; it's the only place you have to live. – Jim Rohn

Day 286

Mindful Eating

Morning Pause: Set an intention to eat mindfully today, savoring each bite.

Noon Pause: During lunch, eat slowly, noticing the taste, texture, and aroma of your food.

Evening Pause: Reflect on your eating habits today. Express gratitude for the nourishment provided.

Classroom Activity: Provide a small piece of food for students to eat slowly, focusing on the experience.

When you eat, appreciate every bite. – Kim Groshek,

Day 287

Gratitude Practice

Morning Pause: Focus on your breath and set an intention to find gratitude today.

Noon Pause: Pause to acknowledge something you're grateful for in the present moment.

Evening Pause: List three things you're grateful for that happened today.

Classroom Activity: Have students share something they're grateful for with the class.

Gratitude turns what we have into enough.– Aesop

Day 288

Setting Boundaries

Morning Pause: Sit quietly and reflect on areas where you need to set boundaries.

Noon Pause: Practice saying "no" to a small request that doesn't align with your values.

Evening Pause: Reflect on your boundary-setting experiences today.

Classroom Activity: Discuss the importance of boundaries and role-play scenarios.

You define how others treat you by what you accept, stop, and reinforce.– Kim Groshek

Day 289

Self-Compassion

Morning Pause: Place a hand over your heart and offer yourself kind words.

Noon Pause: Pause to acknowledge any self-critical thoughts and replace them with compassionate ones.

Evening Pause: Reflect on moments where you showed yourself kindness today.

Classroom Activity: Guide students through a self-compassion meditation.

You, as much as anyone, deserve to live with intention and embrace your full potential. – Kim Groshek

Day 290

Mindful Listening

Morning Pause: Sit quietly and set an intention to listen attentively today.

Noon Pause: Engage in a conversation, focusing entirely on the speaker without planning your response.

Evening Pause: Reflect on your listening experiences today.

Classroom Activity: Practice active listening in pairs, then discuss the experience.

The most precious gift we can offer anyone is our attention.– Thich Nhat Hanh

Day 291

Mindful Movement

Morning Pause: Set an intention to incorporate mindful movement into your day.

Noon Pause: Take a short walk, paying attention to each step and your surroundings.

Evening Pause: Reflect on how mindful movement affected your day.

Classroom Activity: Guide students through a series of gentle stretches with mindful awareness.

Movement is a medicine for creating change in a person's physical, emotional, and mental states. – Carol Welch

Day 292

Mindful Technology Use

Morning Pause: Set an intention to use technology mindfully today.

Noon Pause: Check your devices with full attention, avoiding multitasking.

Evening Pause: Reflect on your technology use today.

Classroom Activity: Discuss the impact of technology on mindfulness and share strategies for mindful use.

Technology is best when it brings people together.
– Matt Mullenweg

Day 293

Mindful Communication

Morning Pause: Set an intention to communicate mindfully today.

Noon Pause: Engage in a conversation, focusing on clarity and understanding.

Evening Pause: Reflect on your communication experiences today.

Classroom Activity: Role-play mindful communication scenarios.

The most important thing in communication is hearing what isn't said.– Peter Drucker

Day 294

Mindful Observation

Morning Pause: Set an intention to observe your surroundings mindfully today.

Noon Pause: Spend time observing nature or your environment, noting details you often overlook.

Evening Pause: Reflect on your observations today.

Classroom Activity: Conduct a nature walk, encouraging students to observe and share their findings.

The more you look, the more you see.– Unknown

Day 295

Mindful Technology Use

Morning Pause: Set an intention to use technology mindfully today.

Noon Pause: Check your devices with full attention, avoiding multitasking.

Evening Pause: Reflect on your technology use today.

Classroom Activity: Discuss the impact of technology on mindfulness and share strategies for mindful use.

Technology is best when it brings people together.– Matt Mullenweg

Day 296

Mindful Listening

Morning Pause: Sit quietly and set an intention to listen attentively today.

Noon Pause: Engage in a conversation, focusing fully on the speaker without planning your response.

Evening Pause: Reflect on your listening experiences today.

Classroom Activity: Practice active listening in pairs, then discuss the experience.

The most precious gift we can offer anyone is our attention. – Thich Nhat Hanh

Day 297

Mindful Movement

Morning Pause (5 min): Set an intention to incorporate mindful movement into your day.

Noon Pause (5 min): Take a short walk, paying attention to each step and your surroundings.

Evening Pause (3 min): Reflect on how mindful movement affected your day.

Classroom Activity: Guide students through a series of gentle stretches with mindful awareness.

Abundance is not something we acquire. It is something we tune into. – Wayne Dyer

Day 298

Loving-Kindness Meditation

Morning Pause: Sit quietly, focus on your breath, and set an intention to cultivate compassion.

Noon Pause: Send loving-kindness to yourself and others.

Evening Pause: Reflect on moments of kindness you gave or received today.

Classroom Activity: Lead a loving-kindness meditation, encouraging students to send goodwill to themselves and others.

Compassion is the basis of morality. – Arthur Schopenhauer

Day 299

Self-Compassion

Morning Pause (5 min): Sit quietly and set an intention to be kind to yourself today.

Noon Pause (5 min): Acknowledge any self-critical thoughts and gently replace them with compassionate ones.

Evening Pause (3 min): Reflect on how you treated yourself today.

Classroom Activity: Discuss the importance of self-compassion and share strategies for practicing it.

You, like everyone else, deserve your own love and affection. – Kim Groshek

Day 300

Empathy Building

Morning Pause (5 min): Set an intention to understand others' feelings today.

Noon Pause (5 min): Engage in a conversation, focusing on truly understanding the other person's perspective.

Evening Pause (3 min): Reflect on your interactions and the empathy you expressed.

Classroom Activity: Role-play scenarios to practice empathetic responses.

When you show deep empathy toward others, their defensive energy goes down, and positive energy replaces it. – Stephen Covey

Day 301

Forgiveness Practice

Morning Pause (5 min): Sit quietly and set an intention to forgive today.

Noon Pause (5 min): Identify any grudges you hold and mentally release them.

Evening Pause (3 min): Reflect on the freedom that forgiveness brings.

Classroom Activity: Discuss the power of forgiveness and guide students through a forgiveness meditation.

Forgiveness is the fragrance that the violet sheds on the heel that has crushed it. – Mark Twain

Day 302

Compassionate Action

Morning Pause (5 min): Set an intention to perform a compassionate act today.

Noon Pause (5 min): Look for opportunities to help or support someone.

Evening Pause (3 min): Reflect on the compassionate actions you took today.

Classroom Activity: Brainstorm ways to contribute to the community and encourage students to participate.

No one has ever become poor by giving. – Anne Frank

Day 303

Compassionate Listening

Morning Pause (5 min): Set an intention to listen with compassion today.

Noon Pause (5 min): Engage in a conversation, listening without judgment or interruption.

Evening Pause (3 min): Reflect on how compassionate listening affected your interactions.

Classroom Activity: Practice compassionate listening in pairs, then discuss the experience.

Listening is an art that requires attention over talent, spirit over ego, others over self. – Dean Jackson

Day 304

Present Moment Awareness

Morning Pause (5 min): Sit quietly and set an intention to stay present today.

Noon Pause (5 min): Engage in an activity, focusing solely on the task at hand.

Evening Pause (3 min): Reflect on moments where you were fully present today.

Classroom Activity: Practice mindful listening and speaking in pairs.

The ability to be in the present moment is a major component of mental wellness. – Abraham Maslow

Day 305

Mindful Listening

Morning Pause (5 min): Sit quietly and set an intention to listen attentively today.

Noon Pause (5 min): Engage in a conversation, focusing entirely on the speaker without planning your response.

Evening Pause (3 min): Reflect on your listening experiences and any insights gained.

Classroom Activity: Practice active listening in pairs, then discuss the experience.

When people talk, listen completely. Most people never listen. – Ernest Hemingway

Day 306

Mindful Movement

Morning Pause (5 min): Set an intention to include mindful movement throughout your day.

Noon Pause (5 min): Take a gentle walk, focusing on each step and your surroundings.

Evening Pause (3 min): Reflect on how mindful movement influenced your day.

Classroom Activity: Guide students through simple yoga poses, emphasizing mindfulness.

Movement is a medicine for creating change in a person's physical, emotional, and mental states. – Carol Welch

Day 307

Mindful Technology Use

Morning Pause (5 min): Set an intention to use technology mindfully today.

Noon Pause (5 min): Check your devices with full attention, avoiding multitasking.

Evening Pause (3 min): Reflect on your technology use and its impact on your mindfulness.

Classroom Activity: Discuss strategies for mindful technology use and create a class agreement.

Technology is best when it brings people together.– Matt Mullenweg

Day 306

Mindful Communication

Morning Pause (5 min): Set an intention to communicate mindfully today.

Noon Pause (5 min): Engage in a conversation, speaking with intention and listening fully.

Evening Pause (3 min): Reflect on your communication and any moments of mindful exchange.

Classroom Activity: Practice mindful speaking and listening in pairs, then share insights.

The most important thing in communication is hearing what isn't said. – Peter Drucker

Day 307

Mindful Observation

Morning Pause (5 min): Set an intention to observe your surroundings mindfully today.

Noon Pause (5 min): Spend a few minutes observing nature or your environment, noticing details you often overlook.

Evening Pause (3 min): Reflect on your observations and any new insights gained.

Classroom Activity: Take a mindful walk around the school grounds, observing and sharing findings.

The more you pause, the more you discover.– Kim Groshek

Day 308

Mindful Journaling

Morning Pause (5 min): Set an intention to journal mindfully today.

Noon Pause (5 min): Write down your thoughts and feelings without judgment.

Evening Pause (3 min): Reflect on your journaling and any patterns or insights.

Classroom Activity: Engage in a group journaling activity, sharing reflections if comfortable.

Journaling is like whispering to one's self and listening at the same time. – Mina Murray

Day 309

Mindful Rest

Morning Pause (5 min): Set an intention to rest mindfully today.

Noon Pause (5 min): Take a short break, allowing yourself to relax without distractions.

Evening Pause (3 min): Reflect on your rest and its impact on your well-being.

Classroom Activity: Discuss the importance of rest and share strategies for mindful relaxation.

Sometimes the most productive thing you can do is relax.– Mark Black

Day 310

Releasing Limiting Beliefs

Morning Pause (5 min): Deep breathing and journaling on limiting beliefs.

Afternoon Pause (5 min): Repeat the affirmation: "I am limitless."

Evening Pause (5 min): Reflect on moments where limiting beliefs surfaced today and reframe them.

Classroom Practice: Encourage students to share one strength they have.

Your beliefs create your reality. Let go of the ones that hold you back. – Kim Groshek

Day 311

The Art of Letting Go & Trusting

Morning: Gratitude meditation focusing on past successes.

Afternoon: List 3 self-imposed limitations and reframe them.

Evening: Visualization of success without barriers.

Classroom: Write down "I can" statements.

Your thoughts shape your reality. Choose them with intention. – Kim Groshek

Day 312

Understanding Surrender vs. Control

Morning: Reflect on a past challenge you overcame.

Afternoon: Write down one small step toward overcoming a current limitation.

Evening: Acknowledge one strength you displayed today.

Classroom: Discuss ways to turn weaknesses into strengths.

Every limitation is an opportunity for growth." – Kim Groshek

Day 313

The Art of Letting Go & Trusting

Morning: Do a Body scan meditation to release tension.

Afternoon: Affirmation: "I trust myself and my journey."

Evening: Identify one belief to release today.

Classroom: Encourage students to share one lesson learned from failure.

Growth starts where comfort ends. – Kim Groshek.

Day 314

The Art of Letting Go & Trusting

Morning: List three things you love about yourself.

Afternoon: Practice saying "I am enough."

Evening: Journal on how self-love can dissolve limiting beliefs.

Classroom: Create a self-affirmation board.

You are worthy as you are, not as you think you should be. – Kim Groshek

Day 315

The Art of Letting Go & Trusting

Morning: Deep breathing to center yourself.

Afternoon: Identify one fear and take a small step to confront it.

Evening: Reflect on moments of courage.

Classroom: Discuss how fear limits growth and how to overcome it.

Fear fades when faced with action. – Kim Groshek

Day 316

The Art of Letting Go & Trusting

Morning: Write a letter to your past self with encouragement.

Afternoon: Practice a mantra of self-compassion.

Evening: Reflect on how your mindset has shifted this week.

Classroom: Have students write letters to their future selves.

Compassion for yourself fuels transformation.– Kim Groshek

Day 317

Understanding Surrender vs. Control

Morning: Breathwork to cultivate calmness.

Afternoon: Identify one area where you're trying to control too much.

Evening: Reflect on where surrender brought positive results.

Classroom: Group discussion on adapting to change.

Surrender is not giving up, but releasing what no longer serves you. – Kim Groshek

Day 318

Understanding Surrender vs. Control

Morning: Journal: What would trusting the process look like for me?

Afternoon: Practice mindfulness while completing a simple task.

Evening: Let go of one worry and focus on the present moment.

Classroom: Talk about an experience where things worked out unexpectedly.

Trust is cultivated in the moments of letting go.– Kim Groshek

Day 319

Understanding Surrender vs. Control

Morning: Meditation on accepting uncertainty.

Afternoon: Take a break and observe nature's natural flow.

Evening: Reflect on an instance when surrendering led to something better.

Classroom: Discuss stories where letting go led to unexpected success.

The unknown is a canvas for infinite possibilities. – Kim Groshek.

Day 320

Understanding Surrender vs. Control

Morning: Affirmation: "I release what I cannot control."

Afternoon: Identify one habit or thought pattern to release.

Evening: Journal about how surrendering feels.

Classroom: Have students identify one thing they can let go of.

Control is an illusion; peace emerges through trust.
– Kim Groshek

Day 321

Understanding Surrender vs. Control

Morning: Visualization of floating down a peaceful river.

Afternoon: Let go of a small responsibility for the day and trust others.

Evening: Reflect on what it felt like to release control.

Release resistance, and let life flow effortlessly. – Kim Groshek

Day 322

Understanding Surrender vs. Control

Morning: Write down areas where you feel resistance.

Afternoon: Choose one and experiment with releasing it.

Evening: Reflect on how releasing changed your day.

Classroom: Discuss how adaptability leads to success.

Adaptability unlocks the power of resilience. – Kim Groshek

Day 323

Understanding Surrender vs. Control

Morning Meditation: Imagine a weight being lifted off your shoulders.

Afternoon: Take a moment to pause before responding to challenges.

Evening: Journal on an unexpected positive outcome from surrendering.

Classroom: Activity where students take turns leading and following.

True leadership is built on trust, and trust begins with the courage to let go.– Kim Groshek

Day 324

Developing Patience in Success

Morning Journal: "What does success feel like to me?"

Afternoon: Walk in nature, focusing on slow, mindful steps.

Evening: Reflect on a time when patience led to rewards.

Classroom: Discuss the importance of delayed gratification.

Success is a marathon, not a sprint. Trust the rhythm of your journey.– Kim Groshek

Day 325

Developing Patience in Success

Morning: Practice slow, intentional breathing for five minutes.

Afternoon: Write about a time when patience led to success.

Evening: Reflect on any impatience today and how you handled it.

Classroom: Discuss the value of patience in teamwork.

Patience is not about waiting; it's about harnessing focused strength.– Kim Groshek.

Day 326

Developing Patience in Success

Morning: Meditate on a visualization of a tree growing slowly but steadily.

Afternoon: Pause before reacting to any challenges.

Evening: Journal about an area where you can cultivate more patience.

Classroom: Have students brainstorm long-term goals and steps to achieve them.

Small steps taken daily create extraordinary achievements. – Kim Groshek.

Day 327

Developing Patience in Success

Morning: List three things in your life that required patience to develop.

Afternoon: Take a mindful walk, focusing on each step.

Evening: Reflect on how patience influenced your interactions today.

Classroom: Activity where students must work on a task that requires patience (e.g., a puzzle).

Trust the process—remarkable things unfold with time. – Kim Groshek

Day 328

Developing Patience in Success

Morning: Repeat the affirmation: "I trust in divine timing."

Afternoon: Identify one rushed decision from the past and what it taught you.

Evening: Journal on how waiting for the right moment benefited you.

Classroom: Discuss historical figures who demonstrated patience in achieving success.

Patience and perseverance hold the power to make obstacles vanish.– Kim Groshek.

Day 329

Developing Patience in Success

Morning: Practice mindful listening in a conversation.

Afternoon: Write down three things you're currently waiting for and reframe them positively.

Evening: Reflect on today's moments of patience.

Classroom: Discuss how patience helps in conflict resolution.

The most valuable things in life are worth the wait." – Kim Groshek.

Day 330

Developing Patience in Success

Morning: Observe something in nature that symbolizes patience (e.g., a flower blooming).

Afternoon: Focus on doing one task at a time without rushing.

Evening: Reflect on how slowing down today impacted your mindset.

Classroom: Have students create a patience timeline for their goals.

Nature does not hurry, yet everything is accomplished. – Lao Tzu

Day 331

How Trusting the Process Fuels Abundance

Morning: Meditation on trusting the unknown.

Afternoon: Identify moments where trust has led to unexpected success.

Evening: Write a letter to your future self with encouragement.

Classroom: Have students create vision boards.

When you trust the process, abundance flows effortlessly. – Kim Groshek

Day 332

How Trusting the Process Fuels Abundance

Morning Affirmation: "I trust in the journey of life."

Afternoon: Write about an instance where trust led to success.

Evening: Reflect on a time you let go and things worked out.

Classroom: Discuss how trust impacts teamwork.

Trust the process, even when the path is unclear. – Kim Groshek

Day 333

How Trusting the Process Fuels Abundance

Morning: Meditation on releasing the need for control.

Afternoon: Take a mindful walk, noticing signs of natural trust.

Evening: Journal about an area where you can practice more trust.

Classroom: Activity on trust-building exercises.

Let go and watch abundance flow. – Kim Groshek

Day 334

How Trusting the Process Fuels Abundance

Morning: Visualize your future self trusting the process.

Afternoon: Identify one area of life where you struggle with trust and brainstorm solutions.

Evening: Reflect on how trusting felt throughout the day.

Classroom: Share experiences of trusting a friend or teacher.

Faith and trust create limitless possibilities. – Kim Groshek

Day 335

How Trusting the Process Fuels Abundance

Morning: Repeat the affirmation: "I am open to receiving."

Afternoon: Practice surrendering a minor decision to intuition.

Evening: Journal on an unexpected blessing from today.

Classroom: Discuss moments when trusting helped solve a problem.

Abundance flows when you release resistance.– Kim Groshek

Day 336

How Trusting the Process Fuels Abundance

Morning: Gratitude practice for everything that has worked out.

Afternoon: Listen deeply without trying to control the conversation.

Evening: Reflect on how trust appeared today.

Classroom: Team exercise on trusting others.

The universe has perfect timing—trust it. – Kim Groshek

Day 337

How Trusting the Process Fuels Abundance

Morning Affirmation: "I embrace uncertainty with confidence."

Afternoon: Let go of one worry and observe the outcome.

Evening: Reflect on how releasing control improved your day.

Classroom: Draw or write about a time when trust led to a positive experience.

Surrender to what is, and magic happens.– Kim Groshek.

Day 338

How Trusting the Process Fuels Abundance

Morning: Focus on deep trust during meditation.

Afternoon: Let someone else take the lead in a task.

Evening: Reflect on how it felt to step back.

Classroom: Role-play trust exercises.

Great things unfold when you trust the flow." – Kim Groshek.

Day 339

How Trusting the Process Fuels Abundance

Morning: List ways trust has improved your life.

Afternoon: Pause before reacting to uncertainties.

Evening: Write about how trust showed up today.

Classroom: Discuss historical figures who exemplified trust.

Trust transforms obstacles into opportunities.– Kim Groshek

Day 340

How Trusting the Process Fuels Abundance

Morning: Breathe deeply and repeat: "I trust the timing of my life."

Afternoon: Let go of a tiny expectation today.

Evening: Journal on unexpected joys.

Classroom: Discuss how trust helps overcome fear.

Everything unfolds in its perfect time." – Kim Groshek

Day 341

How Trusting the Process Fuels Abundance

Morning: Visualize abundance as already yours.

Afternoon: Trust someone else to make a small decision.

Evening: Reflect on any shifts in perspective.

Classroom: Share a time trusting someone benefited the class.

Trust transforms uncertainty into opportunity. – Kim Groshek

Day 342

How Trusting the Process Fuels Abundance

Morning: Affirmation: "I trust in infinite possibilities."

Afternoon: Do something spontaneous.

Evening: Reflect on today's surprises.

Classroom: Group storytelling where each student adds a part without knowing the ending.

Abundance begins where fear fades. – Kim Groshek

Day 343

How Trusting the Process Fuels Abundance

Morning: Express gratitude for unseen blessings.

Afternoon: Let go of control over a small task.

Evening: Reflect on trust's role in today's experiences.

Classroom: Discuss how trust strengthens relationships.

Release, and life rewards you abundantly.

Day 344

How Trusting the Process Fuels Abundance

Morning: Meditate on a symbol of trust (e.g., a flowing river).

Afternoon: Allow someone else to take the lead.

Evening: Reflect in your journal about how trust contributed to today's successes.

Classroom: Share experiences where patience and trust led to positive outcomes.

Life expands when you allow trust in. – Kim Groshek

Day 345

How Trusting the Process Fuels Abundance

Morning Affirmation: "I welcome the unknown with open arms."

Afternoon: Try something outside your comfort zone.

Evening: Reflect on today's growth moments.

Classroom: Encourage students to set a trust-based goal.

Embrace the unknown; it creates space for new possibilities. – Kim Groshek

Day 346

The Power of Presence

Morning: Close your eyes, take 3 deep breaths, and focus on the present moment.

Afternoon: Spend 3 minutes noticing your surroundings—sounds, smells, and textures.

Evening: Reflect on one moment today when you truly felt present.

Classroom: Discuss how being present in small moments can shift daily focus.

***Daily Abundance Quote**: "Success is the sum of small efforts, repeated day in and day out." – Robert Collier*

Day 347

Mindful Breathing

Morning: Practice deep breathing for 5 minutes, focusing on your breath.

Afternoon: Do 3 minutes of diaphragmatic breathing, inhaling through your nose and exhaling through your mouth.

Evening: Spend 5 minutes breathing with gratitude for your accomplishments.

Classroom: Demonstrate how breathing impacts mental clarity and emotional balance.

Daily Abundance Quote: *"Breath is the bridge which connects life to consciousness, which unites your body to your thoughts." – Thich Nhat Hanh*

Day 348

Gratitude Mindset

Morning: List three things you're grateful for.

Afternoon: Pause to acknowledge and feel gratitude in the moment.

Evening: Reflect on a challenge that led to growth.

Classroom: Create a gratitude jar for daily appreciation.

***Daily Abundance Quote**: "Gratitude turns what we have into enough." – Melody Beattie*

Day 349

Setting Intentions

Morning: Set a clear intention for the day.

Afternoon: Reflect on your progress for 3 minutes.

Evening: Assess alignment with your intention and celebrate small wins.

Classroom: Encourage students to set intentions before each class and reflect on them.

Daily Abundance Quote: *"The most important thing is to set your intention, then trust that the universe will support your vision." – Kim Groshek*

Day 350

Self-Compassion

Morning: Check in with yourself, acknowledge emotions, and be kind.

Afternoon: Release negative self-talk, replacing it with kindness.

Evening: Reflect on one way you showed yourself compassion today.

Classroom: Lead a mindfulness exercise on self-compassion.

Daily Abundance Quote*: "Be gentle with yourself. You're doing the best you can." – Unknown*

Day 351

Clearing the Mind

Morning: Sit quietly for 5 minutes, letting distractions drift away.

Afternoon: Take a break, release stress, and focus on your breath.

Evening: Visualize your mind as a calm, ripple-free lake.

Classroom: Lead a mini-meditation to clear students' minds.

Daily Abundance Quote: *"Your mind will answer most questions if you learn to relax and wait for the answer." – William S. Burroughs*

Day 352

Focusing on the Now

Morning: Fully engage in your current activity—eat, walk, or read mindfully.

Afternoon: Take 2 minutes for a mindful check-in, refocusing on the present.

Evening: Reflect on how focus brought clarity to your day.

Classroom: Encourage students to concentrate on one task at a time.

Daily Abundance Quote: *"Focus on the present, and you will create a future that aligns with your highest purpose." – Kim Groshek*

Day 353

Embracing Silence

Morning Pause: Spend 5 minutes in total silence, simply listening to your surroundings.

Afternoon Pause: Take 3 minutes to walk in silence, noticing the sounds around you.

Evening Pause: Reflect on the power of silence to rejuvenate your mind.

Classroom Practice: Introduce silent reflection time in your classroom for 5 minutes to center students.

***Daily Abundance Quote**: "In silence, the soul finds its voice." – Unknown*

Day 354

Mindful Movement

Morning Pause: Engage in gentle stretching or yoga for 5 minutes to awaken your body.

Afternoon Pause: Take a 5-minute walk outside, focusing on the movement of your body.

Evening Pause: Reflect on how your body feels after being mindful in movement today.

Classroom Practice: Introduce a short mindful movement session in your classroom to release tension.

In silence, the soul discovers its authentic voice. – Kim Groshek

Day 355

Releasing Tension

Morning Pause: Start your day by identifying any tension in your body and consciously releasing it.

Afternoon Pause: Pause for 3 minutes and do a quick body scan, releasing tension with every breath.

Evening Pause: Before bed, let go of any lingering tension, focusing on softening your entire body.

Classroom Practice: Lead students in a 3-minute tension release body scan.

Daily Abundance Quote: *"Relaxation is the key to mental clarity." – Kim Groshe*

Day 356

Seeing the Bigger Picture

Morning Pause: Start your day by visualizing a bigger goal and the steps needed to achieve it.

Afternoon Pause: Reflect on how today's tasks contribute to your long-term goals.

Evening Pause: Celebrate the progress made today, even if it was small.

Classroom Practice: Discuss the importance of looking at the bigger picture in learning and life.

Don't watch the clock; do what it does. Keep going.– Sam Levenson

Day 357

Celebrating Small Wins

Morning Pause: Acknowledge one small win from yesterday and appreciate it.

Afternoon Pause: Celebrate any small accomplishment you've made during the day.

Evening Pause: Reflect on how celebrating small wins helps build momentum.

Classroom Practice: Have students share one small win they had today.

Success is a series of small wins. – Kim Groshek

Day 358

Nourishing Your Body

Morning: Start with a glass of water, honoring hydration.

Afternoon: Take a 5-minute break for a healthy snack or water.

Evening: Reflect on your meals and express gratitude.

Classroom: Encourage students to drink water for clarity.

Taking care of your body is an expression of self-love. – Kim Groshek

Day 359

Letting Go of Perfection

Morning Pause: Acknowledge that perfection isn't the goal today—progress is.

Afternoon Pause: Let go of a perfectionist tendency, focusing instead on progress in the moment.

Evening Pause: Reflect on how releasing the need for perfection has made your day lighter.

Classroom Practice: Teach students that mistakes are part of the learning process, encouraging growth over perfection.

Perfection is not the goal—progress is. – Unknown

Day 360

Reconnecting with Nature

Morning Pause: Step outside for a few minutes, appreciating the fresh air and nature around you.

Afternoon Pause: Take a 5-minute walk outdoors, focusing on the trees, sky, or flowers.

Evening Pause: Reflect on how nature rejuvenated your mind and spirit today.

Classroom Practice: Encourage students to step outside briefly to reconnect with nature.

Nature does not hurry, yet everything is accomplished.– Lao Tzu

Day 361

Building Resilience

Morning: Breathe deeply and reflect on past challenges that made you stronger.

Afternoon: Take 3 minutes to recognize your strengths in overcoming obstacles.

Evening: Reflect on today's challenge and the resilience it built.

Classroom: Discuss resilience and share personal experiences.

Resilience is the capacity to recover quickly from difficulties. – Kim Groshek

Day 362

Living with Courage & Inspiring Others

Morning Pause: Set an intention to act with courage today.

Noon Pause: Identify one area in your life where you can take a bold step forward.

Evening Pause: Reflect: What courageous action did you take today, big or small?

Classroom Activity: Courageous Conversations—Students share stories of times they stepped outside their comfort zone.

"Courage starts with showing up and letting ourselves be seen" – Brené Brown.

Day 363

Fostering Creativity

Morning: Spend 5 minutes daydreaming or brainstorming ideas.

Afternoon: Let your mind wander freely to spark creativity.

Evening: Reflect on how creativity helped you see challenges differently.

Classroom: Encourage daily brainstorming for fresh ideas and solutions.

"Creativity is intelligence having fun." – Albert Einstein.

Day 364

Embracing Change

Morning: Journal about a resisted change and reframe it as growth.

Afternoon: Practice five minutes of mindfulness, noticing how change feels.

Evening: Reflect on today's surprises, lessons, and future insights.

Classroom: Discuss growth through change and shifting mindsets.

Change is the only constant in life." – Heraclitus.

Day 365

Embrace Change – Deep Listening

Morning: Listen deeply for 5 minutes and note a standout sound. Express gratitude for growth.

Afternoon: Reflect on today's lesson and list new opportunities.

Evening: Journal about changes and set a confident intention.

Classroom: Discuss growth through change, breakthroughs, and fears.

Embrace change with deep listening—every shift holds the key to growth, if only we take the time to hear it.— Kim Groshek

Final Reflection

The Habits of Wealthy, Mindful Leaders

Reflect: Through intentional pause practices, what changes have you noticed in your joy levels? As you integrate a wealth-building habit, take time to review your finances with calm awareness, setting clear intentions for prosperity, love, and abundance in all areas of your life.

Which practices will you continue beyond your practice in this daily book?
How can you share this practice with others?

Congratulations

You've Completed the 365-Day Pause Power Guide! 🎉

Over the past year, you've taken the time to **pause, reflect, and build confidence**—a true testament to your growth. Remember, confidence isn't a destination; it's a practice. Keep showing up for yourself every day!

What's Next?

✅ **Revisit this guide** anytime you need a reset.
✅ **Inspire others** by sharing what you've learned.
✅ **Keep pausing and stepping into your power!**

Take the assessment quiz to establish your baseline and track your progress. Access your reports here: 👉https://kimgroshek.com/

assessment-report

You are dynamic.
You are unstoppable.
You are YOU.

Epilogue

The Lasting Power of Pause

Living a healthy, balanced, and fulfilling life doesn't have to be complicated. Over the past 365 days, you've discovered the power of **pausing with purpose**—taking intentional moments to reflect, reset, and realign with what truly matters.

This journey was never about adding more to your plate; it was about **simplifying**, creating space for clarity, and allowing abundance to flow naturally into your life. With small, consistent pauses, you have cultivated habits that nurture your well-being, enhance your productivity, and strengthen your mindset.

But this is just the beginning. **Lasting change** is not about a single breakthrough—it's about the daily commitment to pause, listen to yourself, and take aligned action, whether it's setting intentions in the morning, refocusing in the afternoon, or practicing gratitude in the evening, each pause you take fuels your personal growth and transformation.

Now, you hold the tools to live a life of **intentional well-being and success**—a life where pausing is not just a break but a strategy for thriving. The choice is yours: Will you continue to embrace the power of pause?

Pause. Reflect. Grow. Thrive.
With gratitude and abundance, **Kim Groshek**

Kim Groshek, an international best-selling author with over three decades of experience, has shaped industry standards and built $20 billion empires through systematic solutions and intentional living. Her work is invaluable in empowering leaders overwhelmed by demands, helping them overcome obstacles, learn from past experiences, and live their best lives. For thirty years, Kim has inspired leaders to step outside their comfort zones and thrive. To learn more about her work, visit kimgroshek.com.

Books By Author

Now that you enjoyed 365 Days of Pause & Abundance: Practical Daily Tips & Entrepreneurial Wisdom or found it helpful. In that case, I'd genuinely appreciate it if you could take a moment to leave a short review on Amazon. Your feedback helps me continue writing what readers find valuable. You can post your review here: https://amzn.to/48bCpUC

Thanks so much for your support!

Notes

www.ingramcontent.com/pod-product-compliance
Lightning Source LLC
LaVergne TN
LVHW091248150826
845673LV00006B/1353

* 9 7 8 1 9 4 2 6 0 4 6 7 9 *